Sharpening My One-On-One Performance Facilitation & Helping Communication Skills

Helping Customers, Direct Reports, Colleagues and My Boss Succeed

Executing a Performance Facilitating Process and Using My Helping Communication Skills to Help My Customers, Boss, Direct Reports and Colleagues Discuss and Understand Their Challenge(s) and Tap Their Talent to Develop and Execute Solid Plans to Meet the Challenge(s)

Dr. Michael V. Mulligan
CEO Mulligan & Associates

iUniverse, Inc.
Bloomington

<u>Notes</u>

Endorsement

The assessment surveys in this manual will help employees learn where they are functioning as a Performance Facilitator and Helping Communicator. The manual introduces a three stage Performance Facilitation Process and identifies three Helping Communication Skills that employees need to master to help customers, direct reports, colleagues and their boss understand, plan and meet the challenge(s) of the day. This manual is helpful to anyone who manages people and wants to excel as a team unit leader.

Russell Lockridge
Chief Human Resource Officer
Brunswick Corporation

Sharpening My One-On-One Performance Facilitation & Helping Communication Skills
Helping Customers, Direct Reports, Colleagues and My Boss Succeed

iUniverse books may be ordered through booksellers or by contacting:

iUniverse
1663 Liberty Drive
Bloomington, IN 47403
www.iuniverse.com
1-800-Authors (1-800-288-4677)

ISBN: 978-1-4697-7195-3 (sc)
ISBN: 978-1-4697-7196-0 (ebk)

Printed in the United States of America

iUniverse rev. date: 03/15/2012

Helping Skills Are As Important As Technical Skills

The more you work with people, the more important it is to sharpen your performance facilitation behavior and helping communication skills if you are going to help individuals understand their challenge(s) and develop and execute plans to meet the challenge(s). Alan Loy McGinnis[1] who wrote *Bringing Out the Best in People* described two skills that individuals need at various work levels.

Employee Type	Technical Skills	Human Relations/Helping Skills
Rank and File Workers	80%	20%
Supervisors	50%	50%
Executives	20%	80%

Even though the above chart reflects those employees in the rank and file positions need more technical skills and executives need more human relations skills, it is increasingly important that everyone in an organization today develop both skills. If the company expects to be number one in it's industry, sharpening one's performance facilitation and helping communication skills should be promoted as much as developing one's technical skills.

As one takes on the role of a team unit leader, it is imperative that the unit leader has effective One-On-One interpersonal communication skills. The unit leader should be able to function as a performance facilitator and helping communicator and willing to meet face to face with direct reports at least once a month. The unit leader should understand what motivates his/her direct reports and play those strings to help the individual perform up to his/her potential. E-mailing might be good for keeping each other informed but it doesn't help people when they are upset and need to discuss an issue with someone. E-mailing is also not the best way to help individuals understand a problem and make wise decisions and plans to meet a challenge. Does your organization offer a training program that will sharpen your team unit leaders and rank in file workers One-on-One Performance Facilitation and Helping Communication Skills?

Introduction

The goal of this manual is to present the *Performance Facilitation and Helping Communication Model (PFHC Model),* a system that can sharpen the One-On-One *Performance facilitation and Helping Communication Skills* of every employee in the organization. The *Model* has two parts. The **first part** includes a three stage *Performance Facilitation Process.* The **second part** consists of three *Helping Communication* (attending, listening and responding) *Skills* that individuals need to master in order to help others explore and understand their situation and develop and execute action plans to solve a problem or meet the challenge facing them.

If employees can learn the *Performance Facilitation Process* and raise their *Helping Communication Skills* to a high enough functioning level, they can then help customers, their boss, direct reports, and colleagues meet their challenge(s) and be successful. This can be done more effectively in *One-On-One* meetings. Managers and colleagues can help fellow employees understand issues, make better plans and bring out their talent and strengths to achieve their established plan (objectives, strategies and tasks).

There is a strong need for team unit leaders to raise their functioning level as a performance facilitator and helping communicator. A study in March, 2010 by *Career Builder* revealed that 27 percent of 5,700 workers said that they are constantly being bullied by their manager. Bully behavior by unit leaders can build an abrasive and rude culture where employees imitate their leaders.

An article by Sharon Jayson in the August 8th, U.S.A. Today 2011 issue titled *At work, no more Mr. nice guy* reported 75% to 80% of people in the workplace experience incivility. When asked who is to blame, 65% said leadership. 59 % said the employees themselves, 44% said the competition in the work place, 39 % said young adults and 9% said older adults. This study builds a case for all employees sharpening their *Performance Facilitation and Helping Communication Skills.*

When employees are bullied, face an uncivil work environment every day and are put under enormous amounts of pressure to produce results, they can:

- Feel Anxious and Insecure (fearful of losing their job)
- Distrust Management (don't know the truth)
- Feel Abandoned (anaclitic depression)
- Lose Their Incentive to be Creative (why take a chance?)
- Feel that No One Cares About Me as a Person (lack of attention)
- Think about Leaving the Organization (resumes flying out the door)
- Not Become the Best in Their Field (lack a plan and focus)

While senior management needs to meet their business plan, they have to decide how they want to treat their employees to do it. We have developed the *Performance Facilitation and Helping Communication Model (PFHC Model)* to help sharpen the One-On-One *Performance Facilitation and Helping Communication Skills* of all team unit leaders and employees in the organization. The *Model* will help organizations build a humanistic, helping and performance facilitating culture, one that will attract, develop, keep and motivate talent to meet the organization's business objectives. This book includes **four sections.**

In **Section One**, we will assess your *Helping Communication* and *Performance Facilitation Skills* so you know where you are functioning today. We have developed a 30 statement *Helping Assessment Survey* for you to fill out and self score. We also want you to select responses that reflect how you might respond to 10 statements individuals might make to you. You can score the answers and see how you did. Lastly, we want you to fill out the *Performance Facilitator Assessment Survey* and learn how you are functioning as a performance facilitator.

In **Section Two**, we will present *The Performance Facilitation & Helping Communication Model (PFHC Model)*. The Model has two parts. Part one of the Model is *the Performance Facilitation Process*. It contains three stages a helper should take an individual through while helping him/her. The second part of the Model involves mastering three *Helping Communication* (attending, listening and responding) *Skills* which are essential to helping others plan and solve problems.

In **Section Three**, we will identify your functioning level on the *Performance Facilitator Assessment Survey* and *Helping Assessment Survey* and identify where you need to improve and could use some coaching. You will learn how to rate yourself on attending skills and your responses to other people's feelings and messages. We will discuss a rating scale of 1 to 4 with 1 and 2 rating responses being not helpful and 3 and 4 rating responses being helpful. You will learn how to rate your behavior and responses so you can raise your functioning level as a *Performance Facilitator* and *Helping Communicator*.

In **Section Four**, we will discuss how to use the *Performance Facilitation and Helping Communication Model* in One-On One sessions to help customers, your boss, direct reports and colleagues understand their challenge(s) and make and execute plans to meet the challenge(s). We will also review how the *Model* can increase team cohesiveness and team play to meet Plan.

If every employee could raise their functioning level as a *Performance Facilitator* and *Helping Communicator*, you will see team morale, team cohesiveness and team play improve tremendously and individual performances rise to the point that unit and organizational objectives are met and even exceeded.

Notes

Table of Contents

Notes

SECTION ONE

Assessing My Helping Communication

&

Performance Facilitation Skills

Overview of Section One

In Section One, we will ask you to fill out three assessments. In each case, we want you to select your answers based on how you perceive yourself. We want you to be honest so you can learn where you are functioning as a *helping communicator* and *performance facilitator* at this time.

The Helping Assessment Survey

This survey contains 30 statements for you to answer and self score. You will learn your strengths and limitations as a *helping communicator*.

Assessing Your Listening and Responding Skills-How You Would Respond to 10 Comments

We will ask you read a comment that someone is making to you. After you read the comment, review the four responses below and select the one you would most likely make to the person. After you complete this task, you can compare your responses with what we selected as the best responses.

The Performance Facilitator Assessment Survey

We will ask you to review 50 statements that have to do with facilitating performance in others and yourself. Please be honest as you can when selecting the answer that best describes your behavior. You can learn where you are functioning as a *Performance Facilitator* today and where you need to improve for tomorrow.

The Helping Assessment Survey

(Identifying Your Functioning Level)

Please answer the following 30 statements using the scale below. This is not a test with right or wrong answers. It is how you perceive yourself. Please read each of the 30 statements one at a time and put an x by the number that best describes your behavior

Rating Scale-(**Copyright © 2012 Michael V. Mulligan**)
1. This statement is <u>definitely not</u> like me—0% like me
2. This statement is <u>rarely</u> like me.—20% like me
3. This statement is <u>seldom</u> like me—40% like me
4. This statement is <u>somewhat</u> like me—60 % like me
5. This statement is <u>very much</u> like me—80% like me
6. This statement is <u>definitely</u> like me.—100% like me

1. I am objective when someone is talking to me about an issue and my non-judgmental attitude is expressed in my facial expressions and the way I respond.

    6._____5 _____4 _____3 _____2 _____1_____

2. I will not tell individuals what to do after listening to them because my solution might not be right for them.

    6._____5 _____4 _____3 _____2 _____1_____

3. I am recognized as someone who cares about people. I show it through my communication and the way I treat others.

    6._____5 _____4 _____3 _____2 _____1_____

4. I am perceived as a trustworthy and authentic individual. People feel comfortable coming to me to discuss an issue and know what they say will be kept in confidence.

    6_____ 5 _____4 _____3 _____2 _____1_____

5. I work toward creating a common bond with people so they feel comfortable in sharing information about themselves and work with me.

    6_____ 5 _____4 _____3 _____2 _____1_____

6. When I communicate with people, I talk to a person as one adult to another and not like a parent talking to a child.

    6_____ 5 _____4 _____3 _____2 _____1_____

7. I acknowledge people's presence by looking them in the eye, saying hello and calling them by their appropriate name.

    6_____ 5 _____4 _____3 _____2 _____1_____

<u>Rating Scale-</u>(**Copyright © 2012 Michael V. Mulligan**)

1. This statement is <u>definitely not</u> like me—0% like me
2. This statement is <u>rarely</u> like me.—20% like me
3. This statement is <u>seldom</u> like me—40% like me
4. This statement is <u>somewhat</u> like me—60 % like me
5. This statement is <u>very much</u> like me—80% like me
6. This statement is <u>definitely</u> like me.—100% like me

8. I don't twitter and talk on my cell phone when I am in a One on One session or team meeting unless it is relevant to gathering information for the sake of our conversation and making plans.

      6_____5_____4_____3_____2_____1_____

9. I am careful about taking time away from others and myself but I can sense when it is important to take the time to listen to someone.

      6._____ 5_____4_____3_____2_____1_____

10. I am patient when individuals are discussing an important issue. If I am extremely busy at the time, I will schedule a time later in the day to listen.

      6._____ 5_____4_____3_____2_____1_____

11. I know that the first thing about trying to help someone is that you can be harmful as well as helpful.

      6._____ 5_____4_____3_____2_____1_____

12. I know that when someone comes to you for help, they need someone who will listen and help them understand their situation and develop an action plan.

      6._____5_____4_____3_____2_____1_____

13. I know that lay people such as myself can help others as well as professional helpers, especially when discussing and solving normal problems at work/home.

      6._____5_____4_____3_____2_____1_____

14. When someone is talking directly to me or to my group, my eye contact, facial expressions and posture send the message to the person that I am really interested in what you have to say.

      6._____5_____4_____3_____2_____1_____

15. When someone is talking to me I *focus listen* so distractions don't get in the way of my identifying the feelings and message that the person is sending.

      6._____5_____4_____3_____2_____1_____

16. I *respond* very accurately to a person's message to help them understand their situation so they can make wise decisions and plans to solve their problem.

      6._____5_____4_____3_____2_____1_____

1. This statement is <u>definitely not</u> like me—0% like me
2. This statement is <u>rarely</u> like me.—20% like me
3. This statement is <u>seldom</u> like me—40% like me
4. This statement is <u>somewhat</u> like me—60 % like me
5. This statement is <u>very much</u> like me—80% like me
6. This statement is <u>definitely</u> like me.—100% like me

17. When an individual is in a bad mood (mad, hurt or angry about something), I respond with empathy labeling what they are feeling so they can talk their way out of the bad state and into a positive state of mind. This helps them focus and think logically on how to handle what put them in the bad mood.
        6._____5 _____4 _____3 _____2 _____1_____
18. I have developed a broad vocabulary so I can accurately identify what a person is truly feeling.
        6._____5 _____4 _____3 _____2 _____1_____
19. My non-verbal and verbal communication reflects respect for others and shows that I believe in their ability to solve their own problems and issues.
        6._____5 _____4 _____3 _____2 _____1_____
20. When helping an individual, I avoid responding like a *detective* (asking harsh and direct questions—being in control), a *magician* (telling the person the problem will go away) and a *swami* (predicting what will happen if you don't do this) as these roles show disrespect for the person's ability to solve their issue.
        6._____5 _____4 _____3 _____2 _____1_____
21. I always put into practice the *first stage of helping* which focuses on building rapport with individuals. People need to feel comfortable in sharing their feelings and thoughts about an issue. This can be a customer complaining about something or a fellow employee talking about the organization in both a positive and negative way.
        6._____5 _____4 _____3 _____2 _____1_____
22. I build rapport with people by displaying warmth (a smile, a sense of humor and good attending skills), responding with empathy and showing respect. Without rapport, it makes one hesitate to share one's thoughts and feelings on topics.
        6._____5 _____4 _____3 _____2 _____1_____
23. In the *second stage of helping* (exploring, understand and planning), I work with the individual or team of individuals to explore and understand a situation and then develop an action plan (objectives, tasks, strategies) that will help the person/group be successful.
        6._____5 _____4 _____3 _____2 _____1_____

1. This statement is <u>definitely not</u> like me—0% like me
2. This statement is <u>rarely</u> like me.—20% like me
3. This statement is <u>seldom</u> like me—40% like me
4. This statement is <u>somewhat</u> like me—60 % like me
5. This statement is <u>very much</u> like me—80% like me
6. This statement is <u>definitely</u> like me.—100% like me

24. In the *second stage of helping*, I respond with accuracy to what is being said and self disclose past experiences that helps the person or group understand their situation in more depth and then help the individual or group develop appropriate plans.

    6._____5 _____4 _____3 _____2 _____1_____

25. In the *third stage of helping* (action), I push the individual or group to put their plan into action and meet their objectives.

    6._____5 _____4 _____3 _____2 _____1_____

26. In the *third stage of helping*, I work One-On-One with individuals using the *Task Empowerment Process.* I start by identifying the tasks that need to be executed to meet the objectives and plan. I coach the person on the tasks where he/she needs coaching and empower him/her to perform the tasks he/she can do alone.

    6._____5 _____4 _____3 _____2 _____1_____

27 In the *third stage of helping*, I execute the Four M Plan. I will work with individuals and the group to *monitor, modify, measure* results and *meet* the plan (objectives) . . .

    6._____5 _____4 _____3 _____2 _____1_____

28. In the *third stage of helping*, I put into practice constructive positive confrontation. Since I have excellent rapport with individuals, I have earned the right to tell a person that "you are not walking your talk". "You are not doing what you said you would do." This is also a time when I can help a person develop a thicker skin and not be so sensitive.

    6._____5 _____4 _____3 _____2 _____1_____

29. In the *third stage of helping*, I practice intermittent positive reinforcement on individuals. I compliment and give out rewards to individuals when they do excellent work or meet objectives. I reward them in different ways when they don't expect it.

    6._____5 _____4 _____3 _____2 _____1_____

30. I operate as both a counselor (performance facilitator and helping communicator) and as a coach/mentor (teaching individuals how to perform specific tasks). I can help individuals understand and develop plans to solve their own issues and problems.

    6_____5 _____4 _____3 _____2 _____1_____

Calculating your *Helping Assessment Survey* scores

Listed below are *three areas of helping.* There are 10 statements on the survey for each of the three areas. Review each statement on the survey and if you scored a 6, place 15 points by the number below; if your scored a 5, place 12 points by the number below; if you scored a 4, place 9 points by the number below; if you scored a 3, place 6 points by the number below; if you scored a 2, place 3 points by number below and if you scored a 1, place 0 points by the number below. Then add up all the points to learn your total score for that particular area. Place your total score for each of the three areas below to the right and learn the level where you perceive yourself functioning.

Perception of Yourself as a Helper
(Assess Where You Are Today as a Helper)
1_____2_____3_____4_____5_____6_____7_____8_____9_____10_____
Total Score_____

Perception of Yourself as a Communicator
(Reviewing Your Attending, Listening and Responding Skills)
11._____12_____13_____14_____15_____16_____17_____18_____19_____20_____
Total Score_____

Perception of How You Help Others
(Taking a Person from the *Sharing/Rapport Building Stage* to the *Exploration, Understanding* and *Planning Stage* to the *Action/Execution of Plan Stage*)
21._____22_____23_____24_____25_____26_____27_____28_____29_____30___
Total Score_____

	150	120	90	60	30	0	
Perception of Yourself in <u>Three Helping Areas</u>	Definitely Like You 120-150	Usually Like You 90-119	Somewhat Like You 60-89	A Little Like You 30-59	Not Like You 0-29		**Scores**
Perception of Yourself as a Helper	Level 5	Level 4	Level 3	Level 2	Level 1		
Perception of Yourself as a Communicator	Level 5	Level 4	Level 3	Level 2	Level 1		
Perception of How You Help Others	Level 5	Level 4	Level 3	Level 2	Level 1		

Identifying How You Respond to People's Comments

We have provided *10 statements* below that have been made by individuals and we would like you select the responses that best represents how you would respond tothem. We would like you to respond with empathy and to the person's feelings in statements one through five and then respond to the person's message in statements six through *10*. Please put an X by the comment that would best represent your response after you read the statement.

(Copyright ©2010 Michael V. Mulligan)

Statement One—Customer Speaking to You, an Employee

I have been waiting on the telephone for 20 minutes to speak to someone. Why don't you hire more people to service your customers?

1. *It is a busy time of year for us and we are overwhelmed._____*
2. *How can I help You?_____*
3. *I hear what you are saying._____*
4. *It is frustrating to wait a long time when you have other things to do. Let me help you so you can enjoy the rest of your day._____*

Statement Two—Customer Speaking to You, a Salesperson

I have been to four different organizations and you all tell me how great you are and what wonderful services that you offer. Who do I trust and who can I depend on when I need to make some key decisions about what I need to do?

1. *I hear you.. _____*
2. *We really believe we are the best of the best. All our customers are very happy with us. We received a very high customer satisfaction rating last year._____*
3. *Trust is important. You want someone who is honest and really wants to help meet your needs in the short and long run. It does make you question the sincerity of the people doing the talking._____*
4. *You should do your homework and talk to their clients and check every one out with the better business bureau._____*

Statement Three—Unit leader Speaking to another Unit Leader

We are outsourcing too many of our jobs overseas. I am worried that our total facility could be gone in another year and we will all be unemployed. It makes me mad because we have worked so hard to make the organization profitable.

1. *Why are you upset? Our jobs are safe. _____*
2. *I hear you.. _____*
3. *You are concerned for the employees because you have seen how hard everyone has worked to help the organization be successful._____*
4. *We should take the CEO and Board of Directors and tie them to a tree and pound some sense in their heads._____*

Statement Four-Direct Report Speaking to a Colleague

I have had three bosses over the last three years and now I have another new boss. I am anxious about what she is going to be like and what she will expect from me. (**Copyright © 2012 Michael V. Mulligan**)

1. *Quit your whining. I have had five bosses in the last five years.*_____
2. *I hear you. New bosses can be unpredictable.*_____
3. *A new boss can cause you to be very anxious and can cause you to worry about your future with the organization.*_____
4. *Don't worry. You can't control what happens. Just work hard.*_____

Statement Five-Direct Report Speaking to the Boss

Why don't you quit bullying me and the others. You are pushing us too hard.

1. *Are you speaking for yourself or everyone else?*_____
2. *You feel I am pushing you and the others too hard and each person can only take so much of this pace.*_____
3. *Where are you working tomorrow?*_____
4. *I hear you..* _____

Write below the numbers or your answers for each of the five statements.

Statement # One—I have been waiting on the telephone for 20 minutes to speak to someone. Why don't you hire more people to take care of customers?
*Which Number or Response Did You Select?*_____*#4 is the best response*

Statement # Two-I have been to four different organizations and you all tell me how great you are and what wonderful services that you offer. Who do I trust and can depend on when I need to make some decisions about my company?
*Which Number or Response Did You Select?*_____*#3 is the best response*

Statement # Three—We are outsourcing too many of our jobs overseas. I am worried that our total facility could be gone in another year and we will all be unemployed. It makes me mad because we have worked so hard to make the organization profitable
*Which Number or Response Did You Select?*_____*#3 is the best response*

Statement # Four—I have had three bosses over the last three years and now I have another new boss. I am anxious about what she is going to be like and what she will expect from me.
*Which Number or Response Did You Select?*_____*#3 is the best response*

Statement # Five—Why don't you quit bullying me and the others. You are pushing us too hard.
*Which Number or Response Did You Select?*_____*#2 is the best response*

(Next Five Statements-Please respond to the message being sent in statements six through 10.)

We would like you to choose the response that best represents how you would normally respond to the following messages in statements six through 10.

Statement Six—Direct Report Speaking to the Boss

You have put me in a *process improvement program* that is impossible to meet.
You should just fire me now.

1. *I hear you. Don't give up so quickly.* _____
2. *You doubt the process improvement program will treat you fairly and provide you the time you need to improve.*_____
3. *Do you want us to give your severance package and outplacement now?*_____
4. *This is a process the organization put in place to give employees a chance to improve in the areas that are important to succeed in the job. You should be relieved that the organization is giving out mulligans.*_____

Statement Seven-Customer Speaking to You, a Consultant

I have a couple of people on my staff that just keep me awake at night. They never listen to me. They just want to do everything their own way.

1. *What kind of training program did you put them through?*_____
2. *Why don't you fire them and bring in some one who will listen to you?*_____
3. *The independent nature of these individuals are a concern to you because you have a process in place that has worked over the years and they are not following it.*_____
4. *I hear you. What are you going to do about it?*_____

Statement Eight-Colleague Speaking to You, a Colleague

The boss was really in bad mood today. In fact, he/she seems to be in a bad mood almost every day. I hate to be around him/her. I never know if I will get screamed at or patted on the back.

1. *I hear you.*_____
2. *It is like an insane asylum around here. Everyone is on edge.*_____
3. *Your boss is the one who makes you feel secure and safe in your job. When your boss is mad most of the time, it makes you want to hide.*_____
4. *I hate coming to work. I don't work well under fear.*_____

Statement Nine-Direct Report Speaking to You, the Boss

I am getting tired of everyone putting each other down at the meetings. Weneed to come together as a team. You are pitting us against one another rather than building team play.

(Copyright © 2012 Michael V. Mulligan)

1. *I can do what I want to do because I am the boss._____*
2. *I like people competing against one another. Can't you stand the heat?_____*
3. *I hear you knocking but you can't come in._____*
4. *You believe team play is a better way to go than putting teammates against one another._____*

Statement 10-Boss Speaking to You, the Direct Report or Manager

Everyone in this organization needs to step up and be more accountable. Senior management doesn't want to hear excuses, they just want results.

1. Why doesn't senior management get off their high horse and roll up their sleeves and help us in the trenches?_____
2. I hear you. _____
3. Senior management wants everyone to be more accountable and raise their performance level._____
4. Will we receive more pay for this extra pressure?_____

Write below the numbers or your answers for each of the five statements.

Statement # Six—You have put me on a process improvement program that is impossible to meet. You should just fire me now.
Which Number or Response Did You Select?_____#2 is the best response

Statement # Seven—I have a couple of people on my staff that just keep me awake at night. They never listen. They just want to do everything their way
Which Number or Response Did You Select?_____#3 is the best response

Statement # Eight—The boss was really in bad mood today. In fact, he/she seems to be in a bad mood almost every day. I hate to be around him/her. I never know if I will get screamed at or patted on the back
Which Number or Response Did You Select?_____#3 is the best response

Statement # Nine—I am getting tired of everyone putting each other down at the meetings. We need to come together as a team. You are pitting us against one another rather than building team play
Which Number or Response Did You Select?_____#4 is the best response

Statement # 10—Everyone in this organization needs to step up and be more accountable. Senior management doesn't want to hear excuses, they want results
Which Number or Response Did You Select?_____#3 is the best response

If you selected 7 of the 10 best answers, you are responding at a helpful level.

The Performance Facilitator Assessment Survey

Please read each of the 50 phrases and pick the rating scale that best describes you. We will assess you in five areas. There are no right or wrong answers. Copyright © 2012 Michael V. Mulligan

Rating Scale
1. This statement is <u>definitely not</u> like me—0% like me
2. This statement is <u>rarely</u> like me.—20% like me
3. This statement is <u>seldom</u> like me—40% like me
4. This statement is <u>somewhat</u> like me—60 % like me
5. This statement is <u>very much</u> like me—80% like me
6. This statement is <u>definitely</u> like me.—100% like me

(Area One)-Assessing My Behavior as a Performance Facilitator
1. I help customers/fellow employees discuss and understand their challenge(s) (problems, issues and situations) and assist them in developing and executing plans to meet their challenge(s).
   6._____5 _____4 _____3 _____2 _____1_____
2. I am a team maker and not a team breaker.
   6._____5 _____4 _____3 _____2 _____1_____
3. I help fellow employees move from an unpleasant state of mind to a logical or positive state of mind so they can make better decisions and focus on the tasks at hand.
   6._____5 _____4 _____3 _____2 _____1_____
4. I put pep in fellow team member's tanks so they are energized to achieve their assigned tasks. (make compliments, show respect and remain positive and optimistic).
   6._____5 _____4 _____3 _____2 _____1_____
5. I help people identify their strengths/talent and put themselves in the right positions so they can perform at a higher level and help the unit and organization meet it's objectives.
   6._____5 _____4 _____3 _____2 _____1_____
6. I keep myself physically, mentally, morally and spiritually strong so I am on my game and can help others be on their game.
   6._____5 _____4 _____3 _____2 _____1_____
7. I help employees feel comfortable in talking about their mistakes and what they need to do next time to avoid the mistake from happening again.
   6._____5 _____4 _____3 _____2 _____1_____
8. I encourage people to look at the good in each other rather than the bad.
   6._____5 _____4 _____3 _____2 _____1_____
9. I encourage customers and employees to continually communicate with people around them, so everyone remains on the same page and expectations and objectives are met.
   6._____5 _____4 _____3 _____2 _____1_____
10. I am helping to build a caring, performance facilitation and world class organization where people look forward to working with each other on Mondays as well as Fridays.
   6._____5 _____4 _____3 _____2 _____1_____

(Area Two)-Contributing to the Unit/Organization's Business Plan

Rating Scale
1. This statement is <u>definitely not</u> like me—0% like me
2. This statement is <u>rarely</u> like me.—20% like me
3. This statement is <u>seldom</u> like me—40% like me
4. This statement is <u>somewhat</u> like me—60 % like me
5. This statement is <u>very much</u> like me—80% like me
6. This statement is <u>definitely</u> like me.—100% like me

11. I CONTRIBUTE TOWARD THE DEVELOPMENT OF THE ORGANIZATION'S VISION AND MISSION STATEMENTS.

    6._____ 5 _____ 4 _____ 3 _____ 2 _____ 1 _____

12. I CONTRIBUTE TOWARD THE DEVELOPMENT AND ACHIEVEMENT OF THE ORGANIZATION'S OBJECTIVES THAT NEED TO BE MET IN ORDER TO BE THE BEST IN THE INDUSTRY AND PROFITABLE.

    6._____ 5 _____ 4 _____ 3 _____ 2 _____ 1 _____

13. I CONTRIBUTE TOWARD THE DEVELOPMENT AND ACHIEVEMENT OF THE DIVISION AND DEPARTMENT'S OBJECTIVES THAT NEED TO BE MET SO THE ORGANIZATION IS SUCCESSFUL.

    6._____ 5 _____ 4 _____ 3 _____ 2 _____ 1 _____

14. I CONTRIBUTE TOWARD IDENTIFYING THE ORGANIZATION'S CORE VALUES AND MODELING AND LIVING THESE VALUES EVERY DAY AT WORK.

    6._____ 5 _____ 4 _____ 3 _____ 2 _____ 1 _____

15. I CONTINUALLY WORK TOWARD SATISFYING ALL STAKEHODER GROUPS (CUSTOMERS, SHAREHOLDERS, CO-WORKERS, SUPPLIERS, FAMILY MEMBERS, RETIRED EMPLOYEES AND COMMUNITY GROUPS).

    6._____ 5 _____ 4 _____ 3 _____ 2 _____ 1 _____

16. I WORK EFFECTIVELY WITH MY BOSS IN PLANNING, MONITORING AND ACHIEVING THE OBJECTIVES THAT WILL MAKE US LEADERS OR THE BEST IN OUR FIELD.

    6._____ 5 _____ 4 _____ 3 _____ 2 _____ 1 _____

17. I WORK EFFECTIVELY WITH COLLEAGUES AND DIRECT REPORTS TO PLAN, MONITOR AND ACHIEVE THE BEST IN THE FIELD OBJECTIVES THAT WILL MAKE US LEADERS IN OUR FIELD

    6._____ 5 _____ 4 _____ 3 _____ 2 _____ 1 _____

18. I RECOGNIZE THE NUMBER ONE NEED AND OBJECTIVE IS TO MAKE THE ORGANIZATION PROFITABLE SO STAKEHOLDERS WILL BE REWARDED.

    6._____ 5 _____ 4 _____ 3 _____ 2 _____ 1 _____

19. I CONTRIBUTE TOWARD THE RECRUITMENT AND RETENTION OF TALENTED PEOPLE SO THE ORGANIZATION STAYS COMPETITIVE AND HAS THE OPPORTUNITY TO BE PROFITABLE EACH YEAR.

    6._____ 5 _____ 4 _____ 3 _____ 2 _____ 1 _____

20. I CONTRIBUTE TOWARD BUILDING A COLLABORATIVE AND PARTICIPATORY WORK ENVIRONMENT WHERE ALL PEOPLE CONTRIBUTE THEIR IDEAS FOR THE GOOD OF THEIR UNIT AND THE ORGANIZATION

    6._____ 5 _____ 4 _____ 3 _____ 2 _____ 1 _____

(Area Three)-Working One-On-One with My Boss, Direct Reports, Customers/Colleagues

<u>Rating Scale</u>—Copyright © 2012 Michael V. Mulligan
1. This statement is <u>definitely not </u>like me—0% like me
2. This statement is <u>rarely</u> like me.—20% like me
3. This statement is <u>seldom</u> like me—40% like me
4. This statement is <u>somewhat </u>like me—60 % like me
5. This statement is <u>very much</u> like me—80% like me
6. This statement is <u>definitely</u> like me.—100% like me

21. I participate fully in the One-on-One sessions with my boss, direct reports and colleagues to identify, confirm and meet the department and organizations' objectives and vision.
     6._____ 5 _____ 4 _____ 3 _____ 2 _____ 1 _____

22. I am continually developing my attending, listening and responding skills so I can help others (my boss, direct reports, colleagues, customers etc.) understand their challenges, make wise decisions and develop and execute the appropriate plans to meet their challenges.
     6._____ 5 _____ 4 _____ 3 _____ 2 _____ 1 _____

23. I am always working on building a sharing and trusting relationship with my boss, direct reports, colleagues and customers so we feel comfortable in discussing personal issues, mistakes made and developing future strategies.
     6._____ 5 _____ 4 _____ 3 _____ 2 _____ 1 _____

24. I use the *Task Empowerment Process* with my boss and direct reports. We identify the tasks where I and my direct reports need coaching and tasks where we need to be empowered. (left alone to complete the task).
     6._____ 5 _____ 4 _____ 3 _____ 2 _____ 1 _____

25. I developed a *Career Profile* on myself and reviewed it with my boss to identify my strengths and talent so I can be placed in the appropriate position and help the unit succeed. I ask my direct reports to develop a *Career Profile* on themselves as well so I can place them in the right position and use their skills and talent appropriately.
     6._____ 5 _____ 4 _____ 3 _____ 2 _____ 1 _____

26. I completed the *Leadership & Management Analysis Survey* (contains six assessments) and will review the results with my boss to analyze my strengths and weaknesses as a team unit and team member leader and then develop a growth plan.
     6._____ 5 _____ 4 _____ 3 _____ 2 _____ 1 _____

27. I continually discuss the group dynamics of our team with my manager or direct reports so we can facilitate group cohesiveness and team play.
     6._____ 5 _____ 4 _____ 3 _____ 2 _____ 1 _____

28. I continually review the results of my *Self Actualization Needs Assessment Survey* with my manager, meeting my security, safety and social needs so I can become and be the leader I want to be and should be.
     6._____ 5 _____ 4 _____ 3 _____ 2 _____ 1 _____

29. I am continually reviewing the results of my *Route 66 Career Satisfaction Survey* with my manager, and working on the issues that have dissatisfied me so I can be happy in my present position and work environment.
     6._____ 5 _____ 4 _____ 3 _____ 2 _____ 1 _____

30. I AM continually participating in the *Partnership Handshake Program* with my boss making sure 100% of the expectations and agreements between us are met by the end of the year.
     6._____ 5 _____ 4 _____ 3 _____ 2 _____ 1 _____

(Area Four)-Creating a Successful Team Leadership Program

1. This statement is <u>definitely not</u> like me—0% like me
2. This statement is <u>rarely</u> like me.—20% like me
3. This statement is <u>seldom</u> like me—40% like me
4. This statement is <u>somewhat</u> like me—60 % like me
5. This statement is <u>very much</u> like me—80% like me
6. This statement is <u>definitely</u> like me.—100% like me

31. I am constantly promoting a "we" attitude; knowing if the unit (department) and organization succeeds, all of us will succeed.
        6._____ 5_____ 4_____ 3_____ 2_____ 1_____

32. I am committed to motivating myself and teammates to greater heights by using the *Triangle Team Leadership Model: Becoming the Best in Our Field.* (a leadership development and performance management model*).*
        6._____ 5_____ 4_____ 3_____ 2_____ 1_____

33. I am helping everyone in the unit become a leader in their field so the team unit can go faster, farther and higher and be the best in it's field.
        6._____ 5_____ 4_____ 3_____ 2_____ 1_____

34. I work as a team player, overcoming personality and diversity differences, so individual and team objectives are met.
        6._____ 5_____ 4_____ 3_____ 2_____ 1_____

35. I participate in the *Team Knowledge Program* as I want to contribute and learn as much as possible about the organization's plan, my position, functional area and industry to help myself and the unit/organization succeed. (The Team Knowledge Program is where the unit leader asks team members and guesses to talk on certain topics to educate the members of the team).
        6._____ 5_____ 4_____ 3_____ 2_____ 1_____

36. I praise and recognize teammates for their efforts, accomplishments and team oriented behaviors privately and in team meetings.
        6._____ 5_____ 4_____ 3_____ 2_____ 1_____

37. I participate in our team unit's *Gap Closure System*, a process where we write out our objectives and develop action tasks to meet each objective, I and my unit close the Gap of each objective by achieving the tasks we need to complete.
        6._____ 5_____ 4_____ 3_____ 2_____ 1_____

38. I work with my unit to establish a standard of excellence. We identify and master five specific competencies each year so we can become leaders in our fields.
        6._____ 5_____ 4_____ 3_____ 2_____ 1_____

39. I help my unit identify and write our team unit's accomplishments on a *team resume* each month so we know how we are doing as a team. We can then wave our flag to significant others.
        6._____ 5_____ 4_____ 3_____ 2_____ 1_____

40. I work hard on building team cohesiveness and putting enthusiasm and energy in all my teammate's tanks during team meetings so our team can exceed expectations.
        6._____ 5_____ 4_____ 3_____ 2_____ 1_____

(AREA FIVE)—DEVELOPING MY CAREER AND THE CAREERS OF OTHERS

Rating Scale—Copyright © 2012 Michael V. Mulligan
1. This statement is <u>definitely not</u> like me—0% like me
2. This statement is <u>rarely</u> like me.—20% like me
3. This statement is <u>seldom</u> like me—40% like me
4. This statement is <u>somewhat</u> like me—60 % like me
5. This statement is <u>very much</u> like me—80% like me
6. This statement is <u>definitely</u> like me.—100% like me

41. I use a career management model like the *Route 555 Career Management Model* developed by Dr. Mulligan to chart and manage my career journey and then instruct others on how to use the Model. (developing an ongoing *five* year career plan, focusing on *five* career management modules and moving through *five* career transitioning stages).
    6._____ 5 _____ 4 ____ 3 ____ 2 ____ 1 _____

42. I continually fill out the 100 item *Career Competency Survey* developed by Dr. Mulligan and identify where I need coaching in managing my career. I recommend the *Survey* to others.
    6._____ 5 _____ 4 ____ 3 ____ 2 ____ 1 _____

43. I am continually upgrading my *Career Profile* by taking various assessment tools and then targeting positions that match my Profile.
    6._____ 5 _____ 4 ____ 3 ____ 2 ____ 1 _____

44. I am continually developing and executing a *career preparation plan* to help me quality for my next targeted position.
    6._____ 5 _____ 4 ____ 3 ____ 2 ____ 1 _____

45. I am continually keeping my *resume and marketing letters* up to date based on my personal achievements and the achievements of my unit.
    6._____ 5 _____ 4 ____ 3 ____ 2 ____ 1 _____

46. I can execute a *job search process* that will help me obtain an interview in my targeted position either in my organization or another organization.
    6._____ 5 _____ 4 ____ 3 ____ 2 ____ 1 _____

47. I know how to sell myself in an *interview and negotiate* my package so I am hired in my targeted position.
    6._____ 5 _____ 4 ____ 3 ____ 2 ____ 1 _____

48. I work closely with my boss, direct reports and colleagues to make sure we are all successful. I know that by making those around me successful, it will enhance my career down the road.
    6._____ 5 _____ 4 ____ 3 ____ 2 ____ 1 _____

49. I will build a reputation inside and outside the organization through my professional writing and presentations and by being recognized as an expert in my field.
    6._____ 5 _____ 4 ____ 3 ____ 2 ____ 1 _____

50. I will develop my *personal power* (people will want to follow me) and *position power* (empowered) so my value increases with those who can help me advance my career.
    6._____ 5 _____ 4 ____ 3 ____ 2 ____ 1 _____

Calculate Your Scores for Five Performance Facilitation areas

Listed below are *five performance facilitation areas.* There are 10 statements on the survey for each of the five areas. Review each statement on the survey and if you scored a 6, place 15 points by the phrase number below; if your scored a 5, place 12 points by the phrase number below; if you scored a 4, place 9 points on the phrase number below; if you scored a 3, place 6 points on the phrase number below; if you scored a 2, place 3 points by the phrase number below and if you scored a 1, place 0 points by the phrase number below. Then add up all the points to learn your total score for that particular area. Place your total score for each function on the following page and learn the level where you perceive yourself functioning at this time.

(Area One)-Assessing My Behavior as a Performance Facilitator
1_____2_____3_____4_____5_____6_____7_____8_____9_____10_____
Total Score_____ Functional Level _____

(Area Two)-Contributing to the Organization's Business Plan
11_____12_____13_____14_____15_____16_____17_____18_____19_____20_____
Total Score_____ Functional Level _____

(Area Three)-Meeting One-On-One with My Boss/Others to Make and Meet Plan
21_____22_____23_____24_____25_____26_____27_____28_____29_____30_____
Total Score_____ Functional Level _____

(Area Four)-Creating a Successful Team Leadership Program
31_____32_____33_____34_____35_____36_____37_____38_____39_____40_____
Total Score_____ Functional Level _____

(Area Five)—Develop My Career and the Careers of Others
41_____42_____43_____44_____45_____46_____47_____48_____49_____50_____
Total Score_____ Functional Level _____

Go to page 21, write our your total scores and learn where you are functioning in each of the five performance facilitation areas.

Notes

Review Your Functioning Level as a Performance Facilitator

We have combined your 50 answers into five performance facilitation areas. Your total scores should be recorded in the right column below and will place you at one of five functioning levels. The higher your score and level in a particular area, the more you perceive yourself as capable of performing the 10 tasks under that performance facilitation area. The lower your score and level, the less likely you see yourself executing the 10 tasks under the performance facilitation area. <u>Keep in mind that this profile represents the perceptions you have of yourself and is not a test.</u> The score range is 0 to 150.

If you fall at level 5 or at Level 4 with a score of 90 and above, you view yourself as capable of handling most of the 10 tasks included in that performance facilitation area. If your score is 60 to 90 and fall at a 3 level, you see yourself as average in carrying out the 10 tasks under the area. If you fall at Level 2 or 1 with a score of 60 or less, you view yourself as someone who isn't performing the tasks very well in that performance facilitation area. (Copyright © 2012 Michael V. Mulligan)

	150	120	90	60	30	0	Scores
Six Areas	Definitely Like You Scores of 120 to 150	Usually Like You Scores of 90 to 119	Somewhat Like You Scores of 60 to 89	A Little Like You Scores of 30 to 59	Not Like You Scores of 0 to 29	
Assessing My Behavior as a Performance Facilitator	Level 5	Level 4	Level 3	Level 2	Level 1	
Contributing Toward the Organization's Business Plan	Level 5	Level 4	Level 3	Level 2	Level 1	
Meeting One-On One with My Boss and Others	Level 5	Level 4	Level 3	Level 2	Level 1	
Creating a Successful Team Leadership Program	Level 5	Level 4	Level 3	Level 2	Level 1	
Developing My Career and the Careers of Others	Level 5	Level 4	Level 3	Level 2	Level 1	

**"I Know You Believe You Understand
What You Think I Said, but I Am Not Sure You Realize
What You Heard is Not What I Meant"**

Alan Sevehla

SECTION TWO

Reviewing the Performance Facilitation

&

Helping Communication Model

Overview of Section Two

In Section Two, we will present **the Performance Facilitation & Helping Communication Model** (PFHC Model). This *Model* contains two parts. The <u>first part</u> involves the *Performance Facilitation Process* which consists of three stages a team unit leader or employee should take another person through if they are going to help them be successful. The <u>second part</u> of the Model includes mastering three *Helping Communication* (attending, listening and responding) *Skills* which are essential to helping another person understand their situation, develop a plan and use their talent to execute and achieve the plan.

This *Model* is an adaptation of the research that Dr. Robert Carkhuff [2] and Dr. C. B. Truax conducted at the University of Wisconsin at Madison and Dr. George M. Gazda did at the University of Georgia on training lay people to be helpers. Dr. Gazda worked with Dr. Frank Asbury, Dr. Fred Balzer, Dr. William Childress and Dr. Richard Walters[3] and wrote several training manuals that helped employees in the Health and Education fields become effective helpers.

I studied under Dr. Gazda and have counseled and coached over 2,500 business executives and employees. Because of my interest in the business sector, I created the **Performance Facilitation & Helping Communication Model** (PFHC Model) to help business employees become an effective One-On-One *Performance Facilitator* and *Helping Communicator* in their organization. The goal of the *Model* is to raise the functioning level of team unit leaders and employees so they are skillful at helping customers, direct reports and fellow employees succeed.

We will discuss *three important points* that you need to know about helping. First, you can harm someone as well as help them

The first thing that you should know is that how you communicate with a person may be harmful as well as helpful. It just makes good sense if you can help some one, you can also hurt them. The fact is that the things you say and do with someone can make a difference at work and in their life. If what you say to an employee puts them in an angry or distraught state of mind, it will be hard for them to be productive and think logically at work. When I was in my doctoral program, it was reported that more than half the population operate at a harmful level when presented with the opportunity to help someone. If the majority of your team unit leaders are bullies, your organization might achieve it's objectives but at the expense of lowering morale and chasing talented people to the competition. When you review the *Model*, you will learn why team unit leaders need to start in *Stage One* (building rapport) and not *Stage Three* (action and results) where many team unit leaders like to start and remain. Copyright © 2012 Michael V. Mulligan

Second, customers and fellow employees are helped the most when your responses create an in-depth understanding of the situation/problem. They can then develop and execute an appropriate plan to solve the issue/problem.

Your goal is to listen and identify the message and feelings of what a customer or employee is communicating and then makes specific responses back to them that help them understand their situation more clearly. This can help your customers and employees develop the right plan to solve the problem. Premature advice can be harmful and this is done quite often in the work place because everyone is in a hurry. It helps to have an in-depth understanding of the situation and then take the most appropriate action steps to manage the situation.

Third, team unit leaders and employees can learn to help one another as effectively as professionals

Team Unit Leaders and employees can be as effective in helping their fellow employees as professional helpers. For one thing, professional helpers do not have a monopoly on helping. Team unit leaders and employees know the work culture and their industry better and can be just as helpful especially after they have learned *The Performance Facilitation & Helping Communication Model* and mastered the three *Helping Communication Skills*.

The research by Dr. Carkhuff, Dr. Gazda and others discovered that if you were to ask employees in your organization to identify the qualities they seek in individuals in whom they would confide in or discuss something important, the answers you would most often hear would be:

- someone who will listen to me.
- someone who communicates that they care about me.
- someone who won't tell me what to do.
- someone who won't judge me or try to impose his or her values on me.
- someone who will hear what I have to say and not look at their cell phone.
- someone who has a sense of humor.
- someone who will not tell everyone else what we talked about.
- someone who is confident and self-assured and who has his or her act together.
- someone who I trust and will not use the information to get me fired.
- someone who might be faced with the same challenge as I am facing.

What other qualities in a person would you want before you went to them?

Part One of the Model

Executing the Three Stages of the Performance Facilitation Process

If team unit leaders and employees want to be more effective at helping their customers and fellow employees succeed, they need to learn how to execute the first part of the Model, *The Performance Facilitation Process*. Employees have difficulty in working for many team unit leaders because they want to start and remain in Stage Three (action and results). Unit leaders are not use to starting in Stage One (building rapport and a sharing relationship) and then moving to Stage Two (understanding and planning) and then to Stage Three (action and results) because it takes effort and time.

Employees like starting out slow while most team unit leaders want to start out fast. Unit leaders need to understand that they need to build a working and sharing relationship with employees first, a team game plan second and then execute the game plan last.

The three stages of the *Performance Facilitation Process* are outlined below. We will discuss the dimensions in each of the three stages separately and tie them together.

The Three Stages of the *Performance Facilitation Process*		
Stage One **Slow Pace**	*Stage Two* **Moderate Pace**	*Stage Three* **Very Fast Pace**
Building A Working and Sharing Relationship	Dialogue, Understanding and Establishing a Plan	Executing the Plan and Achieving Results
• A Common Ground • Trust • Empathy • Respect	• *Δ Team Leadership Model*-Challenges • *Gap Closure System*-Objectives • *Gap Closure System*—Tasks • *Task Empowerment Process-Prepare*	• Gap Closure System—The 4 M's • One-on-One Meetings • Positive Reinforcement • Constructive Confrontation
Listening		
Attending		Responding
The Three Helping Communication Skills		

Stage One-Building a Working and Sharing Relationship

To be a skilled performance facilitator, everyone in the unit/organization needs to continually build and maintain a working and sharing relationship with each other. Team unit leaders know that building a cohesive team is extremely important, especially after you move into a highly competitive situation that requires team play. The stronger the bond, the better the team will work together to achieve the objective(s). We will now discuss the four dimensions in *Stage One* that will help build strong working and sharing relationships:

- A Common Bond
- Trust
- Empathy
- Respect

A Common Bond

The workforce of America is becoming more diverse each day. Age, sex, nationality, language, values, education and life experience vary in every work environment. The challenge of the organization is to build a common bond that will bring everyone together. This *Model* supports the idea of developing a cause, "Becoming the Best in Our Field" that will excite and unite everyone in the company. Once this common bond is established, barriers will be broken, people will focus on developing and meeting the "Best in Our Field Objectives" and high performance teams will emerge.

The common bond between employees at work should include: **a**) viewing diversity as a strength, **b**) meeting the needs of customers, shareholders, fellow employees and family members, **c**) achieving the department, division and organization objectives to become "Best in Our Industry", **d**) becoming a team builder, **e**) becoming a performance facilitator to help each other grow personally and professionally, **f**) making work a springboard to purpose, success and happiness as one reaches out to help those in one's circle of life, and **g**) helping fellow team members become a leader (the best) in their field so it enhances and advances everyone's career.

In essence, the more you have in common with another individual, the closer you feel to that person no matter what the differences might be. There is an old saying "birds of a feather flock together". You just have to make sure you come up with the same feathers (identifying the one or many things that bond you together).

Trust

In an age of intense competition, "mutual suspicion" has in many cases replaced "mutual" and "reciprocal" trust. Still, mutual and reciprocal trust is the basic ingredient for all honest and effective human relationships. The employer and employee, the customer and salesperson, and members of the same team must be bonded by mutual trust and reciprocal trust or the relationship will not grow.

Mutual trust

People <u>believe</u> in each other. If you are to achieve this relationship with others, then it must begin with you.
1. Mutual trust starts with <u>total honesty</u>, even at your expense. There should be no exaggeration, no cover ups, no distortion and no white lies. It is a contagious characteristic that will spread to others.
2. <u>Admit your mistakes.</u> If you know the other person will admit being wrong, you feel more secure in that relationship.
3. <u>Be sincere</u> when you relate to others. Sincerity instills confidence and builds rapport.
4. Put mutual trust <u>above your own ambition</u> and ego. Suspicion, doubt and envy must be set aside.

Reciprocal Trust

People <u>accept help</u> from those they trust. When the relationship is one of acceptance and trust, offers of help are appreciated, listened to, seen as potentially helpful and often acted upon. An individual accepts help from someone whose perceived motives are congenial to him. We tend to reject offers from people whose offering is seen as a guise for attempts to control, punish or gain power. "Help" is most helpful when given in an atmosphere in which we have reciprocal feelings of confidence, warmth and acceptance. When one feels that his worth as a person is valued, he is able to place himself in psychological readiness to receive help.

A team unit leader can continually measure trust by asking direct reports where they are on the trust scale with each other and with their unit leader. The scale can be 1 to 10 with 10 being high and 1 low. It is important to aim at keeping the mean score of the team unit at 8 and above. You, the team unit leader, can periodically assess where all the team members are on the trust scale by asking them to give you a number on the trust scale. The rating scale numbers can be collected without names on them. The unit leader can determine a mean score on himself/herself and the members and develop a plan to increase trust.

Empathy

Empathy is the key condition in developing close relationships and helpful communication with another person. Not only must another person's feelings be understood, but this understanding must be put into words to that individual.

The *first step* in communicating with empathy is to listen carefully to what an individual is saying about how they feel as a result of what is happening to them. The *second step* is thinking of words that represent the person's feelings and situation. The *third step* is to respond using the words that accurately describe how the individual is feeling.

Empathy and sympathy are different. An expression of sympathy usually tells the person you are sorry about their situation or what has happened to them. It communicates: "I feel bad for you." You have to be careful with sympathy statements because the receiver might interpret your message as saying "I feel sorry for you". This type of statement can make a person angry because they don't want anyone to feel sorry for them. An empathetic statement shows more respect to the person than a sympathetic statement.

When we respond with empathy, we show that we understand what someone is truly feeling. Some people try to take a shortcut and say, "I know what you mean," or "I hear you." Those types of phrases are used because people might not really know how a person is really feeling and it is an easy statement to make. To really help someone understand their feeling, you have to put a label on the feeling.

The helpfulness of empathic responding knows no bounds. The more you can label the feelings of a person in an accurate way, the more a person feels you understand them. It can build meaningful relationships and most of all it is a way to take a person from an angry or bitter state to one that is natural and positive. It provides an opportunity for a person to work through anger, fear, and hurt and move into a logical state of mind where they can make wise decisions and be more productive.

How many bad decisions have people made at work because they were angry or mad at someone. When a person makes important decisions, he/she should be in a logical state of mind and not one of anger. Employees can help fellow employees stay positive and make wise decisions.

Respect

Respect is another key condition to being an effective *Performance Facilitator* and *Helping Communicator*. Respect is the belief we have in another person's worth and potential. We demonstrate respect by good attending behavior and showing our confidence in another person's ability to solve his/her own problems. We do this by supporting their efforts rather than doing things for them.

It means communicating as one adult to another and not acting as parents telling their children what to do. To show respect to a person, you should be non-judgmental and have unconditional/positive regard for the person, even if he fails once or twice. The person's effort and ability to perform tasks play a part in how we view one another. There are five communication styles or roles people play below that show disrespect to individuals. These styles show disrespect because they don't help the individual solve his or her own situation or problem.

#1-The detective role—This individual is eager to track down the facts of the situation and grills you about the details of what happened. The detective controls the flow of the conversation and puts people on the defensive. He is more interested in finding answers than helping the individual solve his/her own problem or situation.

#2-The magician role—This individual makes the problem you have described disappear just like they would make a bunny disappear in a hat. The magician says the problem will eventually take care of itself so there is no need to discuss it. The magician denies the importance or real existence that there is a problem which doesn't validate what you are feeling and seeing for yourself.

#3-The foreman role—The foreman, who is pushing for productivity, believes if you are kept busy you want think about the problem. It is telling you that completing the assigned task is more important than your problem. In essence, hard work will make you forget about your problem.

#4-The swami role—The swami guesses and predicts exactly what is going to happen. By declaring the forecast, you are relieved of responsibility and you can sit back and let the prophecy come true. This person knows everything.

#5-The sign painter role—The sign painter thinks your problem can be solved by putting a name on it. The sign painter has an unlimited inventory of labels to affix to a person and their problem. This person attempts to identify the problem but not help you solve it.

Stage Two-Dialogue, Understanding and Establishing a Plan

The four dimensions of the *Second Stage* include:

- The Δ Team Leadership Model: Becoming the Best By Meeting Challenges
- The Gap Closure Model: Establishing Objectives to Meet Challenges
- The Gap Closure Model: Identifying the Tasks that will Meet the Objectives
- (Close the Gap of Each Objective from where you Start and End)
- The Task Empowerment Process-Building Expert Leaders in their Field

The Δ Team Leadership Model: Becoming the Best By Meeting Challenges

The Δ_**Team Leadership Model: Becoming the Best by Meeting Challenges** is a leadership development and performance management system that can help team unit leaders transform their direct reports into leaders in their field and the unit into the best in it's industry. An individual or group needs to identify the challenge(s) and then establishes objectives that if met would meet the challenge(s). If the objectives are clear, believable, achievable and monitored closely, the *objectives* and challenges will be met. When looking at the Triangle, the team unit leader is placed at the bottom of the triangle which signifies the support for the team. The unit is stationed on the left side of the triangle and the team members are on the right side. The words "Becoming Leaders in Our Field" are on the inside of the Triangle. During the One-On-One sessions, the unit leaders will help direct reports manage personal issues and focus on completing their assigned tasks to meet their objectives and the unit's objectives. If everyone meets their individual objectives, the unit and organization objectives, the challenges should be met.

Challenges (meeting objectives) are what an organization, division, department and individual face on a day-to-day basis. Some challenges are more serious than others. As a skilled helper/performance facilitator, we need to be sensitive and know when the problem or challenge is critical and needs more time to be discussed. If we know the issue is important, then we should take the time to be attentive, listen and respond to help individuals or the group develop action tasks to solve the problem or meet the challenge at that time.

If it is a deep personal problem that someone is experiencing and you don't have the time at that point in the day to be attentive, defer the issue to a point during the day when you have the time to listen. If you feel uncomfortable with helping the person solve his/her personal problem, suggest they go to the employment assistance program (E.A.P.) to discuss the situation. Whether you are in an important meeting with ten people or a session with one person, the key is excellent attending, listening and responding skills to increase understanding so better planning and decisions can be made to meet the challenge.

The Gap Closure System-Establishing Objectives to Meet Challenges

The *Gap Closure System* is an approach that helps individuals and team units understand where they are today and where they need to be tomorrow in order to meet challenge(s) and be successful. Individuals and groups analyze their challenges and then establish objectives that need to be met to meet them. The *Gap Closure System* is a simple planning process that team unit leaders can use with their direct reports to analyze where they are today, determine where they need to be tomorrow and identify what they need to do to get there. Some example objectives would include:

1. We need to increase our truck sales from $5 billion to $6 billion dollars starting January 1, 2012 and concluding on December 31, 2012.
2. We need to reduce our expenses in our department from $2 million to $1.8million starting January 1, 2012 and concluding December 31, 2012.
3. We need as a team to raise our functioning level as a Performance Facilitator and Helping Communicator from a mean score of 2.0 to 3.0 starting January 1, 2012 and concluding December 31, 2012.
4. We need to lose weight in our department from a mean of 210 lbs to a mean of 190 lbs starting January 1, 2012 and concluding December 31, 2012.
5. We need to raise our customer satisfaction score of 75% to 90% starting January 1, 2012 and concluding July 1, 2012.
6. We need to help you to move from being in very mad state to a logical not mad state of mind. You can use the scale of 1 (very mad) to 10 (not mad). It is difficult to quantify an objective like this one so you would have to ask the person to describe their feelings using the 1(very mad) to 10 (not mad) scale.

The Gap Closure System-Establishing Tasks to Meet Objectives

As you or your team unit establishes an objective that needs to be met to meet a challenge, you then need to identify tasks that need to be executed to help meet the objective or close the Gap. An example of an objective is given below.

1. **Objective**—Our team unit will lose weight from a mean *sco*re of 210 lbs (the average weight of 10 people in our department) to a mean score of 190 lbs starting January 1, 2012 and concluding December 31, 2012.
   (*Team Unit Tasks*)
   Task # One—Each person on the team needs to lose 20 pounds in 12 months.
   Task # Two—Each person on the team needs to lose 1.75 lbs each month.
   (Individual Tasks)
   Task #One—Each member on the team will attend the meetings at weight watchers for one year.
   Task # Two-Each person on the team will not have anything to eat after 8pm.

The Task Empowerment Process (TEP)—A Five Step Process

The *Task Empower Process* is a process that unit leaders can use in One-On-One sessions to help their direct reports establish and execute tasks to meet objectives (challenges). This <u>five step</u> program is meant to help individuals execute all their assigned tasks in an expert manner so the gaps in the *Gap Closure System* are closed or the objectives are met by the dates that were established.

In the *first step*, the unit leader and direct reports identify the tasks that need to be met to help achieve a specific objective in the *Gap Closure System*.

In the *second step*, the direct report and unit leader identifies the tasks where coaching is needed and those tasks that he/she can do alone.

In the *third step*, the Team Unit Leader empowers the direct report to perform the tasks that he/she can do alone to meet the objective.

In the *fourth step*, the Team Unit Leader will coach the direct report on the tasks where he/she needs coaching.

In the *fifth step*, the direct report is empowered to perform the remaining tasks. This means the direct report at this time is an expert in performing all the tasks that have been assigned to him/her and should be able to meet his/her objectives and help the unit meet it's objectives.

Stage Three-Executing the Plan and Achieving Results

Once you have identified your objectives and the tasks each direct report needs to achieve to meet the predefined objectives, you will move into *Stage Three*, Executing the Plan and Achieving Results. The four conditions of *Stage Three* include:

- The Gap Closure System-The Four M's
- One-on-One Meetings
- Constructive Confrontations/Immediacy
- <u>Positive Reinforcement Communication</u>

<u>The Gap Closure System-The Four Ms</u>

As unit leaders and direct reports begin to execute the action plans (tasks) you will:

— *Monitor* how direct reports are executing their tasks
— *Measure* the direct report's efforts and results
— *Modify* individual tasks based on meeting unit objectives
— *Meet* individual and the unit's objectives (*Close the Gap*).

<u>One-on-One Meetings</u>

Unit leaders will meet with their direct reports and boss once a month discussing the *Four M's*, confronting and providing positive reinforcement to each other. The One-On-One sessions will keep everyone focused on what needs to be accomplished to meet the objectives and *Close the Gaps*.

The One-On-One meetings will help unit leaders manage their direct reports more effectively. If a direct report has a personal issue at home or with a fellow worker, you can discuss the situation One-On-One with him/her. If two direct reports are going after each other in a harmful way during team meetings, you can talk to each of them alone and point out that their behavior is destructive to the good of the team as well as their working relationship. It is difficult to solve these type of problems during a team meeting. You always want to save face for each individual.

Constructive Confrontation/Immediacy

The word "confrontation" is often associated with the stripping away of a person's defenses and brutally exposing his or her weaknesses. The *Performance Facilitator & Helping Communication Model* advocates a constructive confrontation. It is not punitive and cruel. Constructive or performance facilitating confrontation helps the individual examine the inconsistencies in his/her work/life and to make better use of personal strengths and resources.

The focus is on appropriate behavior and not the person. Confrontation without an established working relationship is rarely helpful. The model emphasizes that you must earn the right to confront and this is done through building relationships. This is why we say team unit leaders need to start in *Stage One* of the *Performance Facilitation Process* and move to *Stage Three* after strong relationships have been formed. Confrontation can be damaging creating high levels of anxiety in a person.

Immediacy represents the working relationships you have at the moment with an individual. If you have a good working relationship, it is easier to use constructive confrontation to point out discrepancies between what a person says he/she is going to do and what he/she actually does.

Positive Reinforcement Communication

Just as it is important to point out discrepancies in performance, it is important to recognize excellent work and provide positive feedback on a timely basis. When an individual completes a task or project, meets predetermined objectives or behaves in a certain way to facilitate performance in others, the person should be complimented or recognized. Positive reinforcement should be done on an intermittent basis. This means people should be rewarded or praised at different times without expecting it. If we reward or praise someone all the time, it doesn't mean as much. The problem is that people aren't praised or recognized enough and especially at the right times.

Part Two of the Model

The Three Helping Communication Skills

To function at a helpful level, one needs to master the following three Helping *Communication Skills* and be able to use them in all *Three Stages* of the *Performance Facilitation Process*. The three skills include:

- **Attending Skills**

- **Focus Listening Skills**

- **Accurate Responding Skills**

Attending Skills

Attending skills represent the non-verbal behavior or physical gestures you reflect while listening to another speak. These behaviors, such as facial expressions, eye contact, mannerisms, movement and posture carry messages to persons with whom you talk. Your physical responses reflect your interest in others, respect and how much you care for them. Your attending skills can send the message to others that you care for them or don't care for them as a person.

Attending skills include non-verbal communication, body language and warmth. Non-verbal communication represents at least 70% of the communication between people. If your physical gestures show interest in what other individuals are saying in One-On-One and team meetings, it will make everyone on the team feel important and will reinforce sharing. If your eyes are elsewhere when someone is speaking or you are texting, it makes the person feel what he/she is saying is not that important. This shows disrespect to the individual.

The five attending skills that you need to focus on include your:
- Facial expressions
- Eye contact
- Mannerisms and gestures
- Space
- Posture

Focus Listening Skills

Focus listening takes a lot of energy and commitment and is very difficult for most people to do. Some of the reasons we are not good listeners are:

1. We are pre-occupied in thought. We might be thinking of the project or task we have to get done by 5 p.m. We also could be thinking of something that happened a few hours ago that was distressing and we can't get it out of our minds. There are many things that can distract us.
2. We are thinking about what we are going to say and not concentrating on what others are communicating. If we feel that we are going to be evaluated every time we say something in a meeting, we most likely will concentrate on what we are going to say rather than listening to others.
3. We might not care for the person talking or the subject matter being discussed. If we dislike or are prejudiced toward a person, we are less likely to listen to what that individual has to say. In addition, if we don't know or care much about the subject being discussed, we can easily tune out.
4. We don't know what to concentrate on when a person is talking to us. A focused listener should concentrate on two areas.

   - Understanding the person's feelings and mood based on his/her words and tone of voice.
   - Understanding the person's message or what he/she is really saying.

We use the terminology *focused listening*, because one has to really concentrate on what a person is saying if he/she is to truly understand the individual's message and feelings.

Very often you will hear spouses say, "My husband/wife just doesn't listen to me." The problem is that an individual needs to clear everything out of their head and prepare themselves to be a good listener. Dr. Michael Mulligan, a former catcher in baseball, gives the example of pitching to the catcher. When the pitcher gets ready to throw his next pitch, the catcher has to be in a special crouch and prepared to catch the pitch. If the catcher is not concentrating on the type and the speed of the pitch, the ball could hit the catcher some place other than the mitt. This could hurt the catcher just as well hurt the person who is not focusing on what the boss is saying at a meeting. One has to concentrate and be ready if the ball/message is to be received cleanly/clearly.

Accurate Responding Communication Skills

To be a highly skilled helping communicator, it is important that your response hits the target so it helps to increase understanding. If you are discussing a particular problem with your doctor and the doctor doesn't respond accurately to what you said to clarify what the problem is at this time, the wrong medication can be relayed to the pharmacist. The medication or action prescribed can cause great damage to that person if the prescription is wrong.

Most people are ineffective at accurately responding. They don't listen long enough to gain a clear picture of the problem, and their response will generally miss the target. This is where a person can take the conversation of someone in another direction. However, the person speaking should learn how to keep their remarks to the point, and not ramble. This can help the listener. A long speech can cause another person's mind to fall asleep after three minutes. You should try to promote ongoing interaction between you and others. The sound of one's own voice wakes the mind up and keeps it alert.

Accurate responding communication is listening to what a person is saying and feeding back what has been said in a descriptive manner. This enhances the understanding of the situation or problem. If we communicate on target, we increase understanding. If our communication misses the target, we decrease understanding and this can impact the decision making process in a negative way.

Three important factors in accurate responding include:

1. Not interrupting others but truly listening to their message and feelings.
2. Broadening your vocabulary with feeling words so you can respond with words that accurately describes one's feelings and situations.
3. Working on the tone and loudness of your voice, so you can send the "appropriate" message.

If you want yourself and others to go through a training program to become a more effective *Performance Facilitator* and *Helping Communicator*, please call Mulligan and Associates Inc. at 847 981-5725

SECTION THREE

Raising My

Performance Facilitation

&

Helping Communication
(Attending, Focus Listening & Accurate Responding)

Functioning Level

Overview of Section Three

In *Section Three*, our goal is to help you take a step forward in raising your performance facilitation and helping communication functioning level. We will do this by focusing on where you are functioning as a *Performance Facilitator* and *Helping Communicator* now and where you need to improve to be more helpful to others in the future. We will cover the following topics.

- Definition of a Performance Facilitator
- Reviewing Your *Performance Facilitator Assessment Results* and Identifying Where You Need to Improve or Need Coaching.
- Reviewing *Your Helping Assessment Survey Results* and Identifying Where You Need to Improve or Need Coaching
- Reviewing the *Overall Helping Communication Response* Rating Scale
- Sharpening My Attending Skills When Listening to a Person Speak
- Listening/Responding with Respect and Accuracy to a Person's Feelings
- Listening/Responding with Respect and Accuracy to a Person's Message

(Definition of a Performance Facilitator)

<u>Performance</u> is defined as showing progress from where you were yesterday to where you are today and usually has metrics that can point out the progress made.

Performance can mean different things to people. For example, one can be in an accident at work and be told he/she might not walk again. By going through physical therapy, a person can gradually walk again but it will mean taking progressive steps. Another example of performance that we don't think about much is the mental attitude one brings to work. If you continually have a negative attitude about the people you work for and with, it will show in your behavior and results. If someone constantly has a bad attitude at work, a colleague or boss needs to sit down with that person One-On-One and let them talk about and understand why they are so mad or upset. Then they can execute a plan that will help them develop a positive attitude and thicker skin when being criticized.

The definition of performance that the majority of us understand is developing standards (quality and quantity) and objectives and identifying and completing tasks that meet the pre-determined standards and objectives. Objectives define what is to be accomplished and have a starting and ending date. You use metrics to determine if you met the performance expectations.

<u>A facilitator</u> helps individuals move forward to perform specific tasks that will meet their predetermined standards and objectives. It includes sharpening one's expertise in attending, listening and responding so you can help individuals understand their situation in-depth, make and execute plans and achieve results.

In essence, a <u>performance facilitator</u> works with an individual One-On-One and helps them identify their challenge(s) and develop and execute a plan to meet the challenge(s). You help people grow by letting them operate as a self manager.

Sociologists and psychologists have stated that in our lifetime, most of us will only develop 10 to 15% of our potential. Dr. Michael V. Mulligan met with over 2,500 executives, managers and non-exempts One-On-One during a 28-year span and came up with his six factor performance theory:

The six factors that impact your performance or potential at work include:
- Yourself
- Your manager
- Your manager's supervisor
- Your direct reports
- Your co-workers
- Your relationship with your family or significant other

<u>Factor #1—Yourself:</u> You have to take charge of your career by continuing to learn about yourself. It is important that you are aware of your sensitivity threshold, interests, personality, skill set, values, talent, capabilities and the various levels of pressure you can handle. The understanding of self and the world of work helps you place yourself in the right position and company so you can grow and be successful. By knowing yourself and developing your position and personal power, you can better direct, market and manage your career. Your boss and team mates can help you become a leader in your field if you work with them.

<u>Factor #2—Your Manager:</u> If your manager believes his/her main goal is to develop the potential in you and the other direct reports, you have someone who knows his/her role. The first priority of a good manager is to spot and develop talent and use it in the appropriate places in the unit/company. The second priority is to make sure direct reports know what is expected of them. Much research has pointed out that performance and job satisfaction is directly related to the relationship and communication between an individual and his/her manager. The more quality meetings you have with your manager One-On-One, the more he/she can help you develop your strengths through talent and performance management.

Most of the 2,500 individuals who met with Dr. Mulligan told him that they were in a One-On One meeting with their manager twice a year, once in the beginning and at the end to receive performance reviews which tied into bonuses and next year's salary. They never received feedback on how they were doing until they met at the end of the year. This raises the question as to why unit leaders don't meet One-On-One with their direct reports more often?

Factor #3—Your Unit Leader's Supervisor: If your unit leader's supervisor emphasizes effective One-On-One sessions and builds high-performance teams, your manager will spend more of his time with you and others to develop you as a leader. The behavior of your manager often reflects the attitude of his/her supervisor.

Factor #4—Your Colleagues: If your colleagues behave as performance facilitating partners, you will create a motivational environment. Colleagues can play a major role in each other's growth and development. Individuals should think of the competition as being outside of the company rather than inside of it. A collaborative and cooperative work structure should be created in every department and throughout the organization. Research shows that people who trust and like working with you will come looking for you when they move up the career ladder.

Factor #5—Your Direct Reports: If you are the manager, your goal is to select and retain people who will help you and others become leaders in your field and the department a championship team. The more your direct reports grows as leaders, the more the organization will grow.

The quality and frequency of the One-on-One sessions between you and your direct reports will determine individual performance plus whether or not your department and company meet it's objectives. A professional relationship, excellent communication, strong ties and ongoing planning meetings between you and your direct reports will increase trust, team play, focus on the objectives, productivity, performance, loyalty, morale, risk-taking, effort, wellness, enthusiasm, retention and the chance to be successful.

Factor #6—Your Relationship with Your Family or a Significant Other: If you receive love, support and positive reinforcement from your family or significant other, you will bring a positive attitude to work. This attitude will help you focus, be more productive and perform at higher levels. At the same time, if you are appreciated and recognized for your achievements at work, you will take a positive attitude home with you.

"If you treat a person as they are, they will remain as they are. But if you treat a person as they ought to be and should be they will become what they ought to be and should be".—Goethe

Raising My Performance Facilitation Functioning Level

Review Your *Performance Facilitator Assessment Survey Results.* Please go to page 21 in this manual and place your scores below in the proper categories and learn at what level you functioning in that particular area.

If you fall at level 5 or at Level 4 with a score of 90 and above, you view yourself as capable of handling most of the 10 tasks included in that performance facilitation area. If your score is 60 to 90 and fall at a 3 level, you see yourself as average in carrying out the 10 tasks under the area. If you fall at Level 2 or 1 with a score of 60 or less, you view yourself as someone who isn't focused on or performing the tasks in that performance facilitation area. At what level are you functioning in each of the six categories?

(Copyright © 2012 Michael V. Mulligan)

150	120	90	60	30	0		
Six Areas	**Definitely Like You Scores of 120 to 150**	**Usually Like You Scores of 90 to 119**	**Somewhat Like You Scores of 60 to 89**	**A Little Like You Scores of 30 to 59**	**Not Like You Scores of 0 to 29**	**Scores**
Assessing My Behavior as a Performance Facilitator	Level 5	Level 4	Level 3	Level 2	Level 1	
Contributing Toward the Organization's Business Plan	Level 5	Level 4	Level 3	Level 2	Level 1	
Meeting One-On One with My Boss and Others	Level 5	Level 4	Level 3	Level 2	Level 1	
Creating a Successful Team Leadership Program	Level 5	Level 4	Level 3	Level 2	Level 1	
Developing My Career and the Careers of Others	Level 5	Level 4	Level 3	Level 2	Level 1	

Identify Where You Need to Improve

Review the 10 Statements under Each of the Six Performance Facilitator Areas and Identify the Behaviors Where You Need to Improve or Need Coaching

Assessing My Behavior as a Performance Facilitator

My Contribution toward the Organization's Business Plan

Meeting One-On One with My Customers, Direct Reports and Others

Creating a Successful Team Leadership Program

Developing My Career and the Careers of Others

Raising My Helping Communication Functioning Level

Review Your *Helping Assessment Survey Results.* Please go to page 9 in this manual and place your scores for the three helping areas below in the proper categories and learn the level which you functioning in that particular area.

If you fall at level 5 or at Level 4 with a score of 90 and above, you view yourself as capable of handling most of the 10 tasks included in that performance facilitation area. If your score is 60 to 90 and fall at a 3 level, you see yourself as average in carrying out the 10 tasks under the area. If you fall at Level 2 or 1 with a score of 60 or less, you view yourself as someone who isn't performing the tasks in that performance facilitation area. At what level are you functioning in each of the three helping areas?

(Copyright © 2012 Michael V. Mulligan)

	150	120	90	60	30	0	
Perception of Yourself in Three Helping Areas	**Definitely Like You** 120-150	**Usually Like You** 90-119	**Somewhat Like You** 60-89	**A Little Like You** 30-59	**Not Like You** 0-29		Scores
Perception of Yourself as a Helper	Level 5	Level 4	Level 3	Level 2	Level 1		
Perception of Yourself as a Communicator	Level 5	Level 4	Level 3	Level 2	Level 1		
Perception of How You Help Others	Level 5	Level 4	Level 3	Level 2	Level 1		

Identify Where You Need to Improve

Review the 10 statements under each of the three *helping areas* and identify the behaviors where you need to improve or need coaching

Perception of Yourself as a Helper

Perception of Yourself as a Communicator

Perception of How You Help Others

Reviewing Your Responses to 10 Statements

Review the *empathy responses* you selected on pages 10 and 11 of this manual and write your answers below. How many did you select that were identified as the best responses?_____

Statement # One—I have been waiting on the telephone for 20 minutes to speak to someone. Why don't you hire more people as I pay enough for service.
*Which Number or Response Did You Select?*_____*#4 is the best response*

Statement # Two-I have been to four different organizations and you all tell me how great you are and what wonderful services that you offer. Who do I trust and can depend on when I need to make some decisions about my company?
*Which Number or Response Did You Select?*_____*#3 is the best response*

Statement # Three—We are outsourcing too many of our jobs overseas. I am worried that our total facility could be gone in another year and we will all be unemployed. It makes me mad because we have worked so hard to make the organization profitable
*Which Number or Response Did You Select?*_____*#3 is the best response*

Statement # Four—I have had three bosses over the last three years and now I have another new boss. I am anxious about what she is going to be like and what she will expect from me.
*Which Number or Response Did You Select?*_____*#3 is the best response*

Statement # Five—Why don't you lay off me and the others. You are pushing us to hard.
*Which Number or Response Did You Select?*_____*#2 is the best response*

Hopefully, you selected the five best responses. We will discuss the rating scale for *empathy response* **statements in this section.**

Review the *content or message responses* you selected on pages 12 and 13 of this manual and write your answers below. How many did you select that were identified as the best responses?_____

Statement # One—You have put me on a process improvement program that is impossible to meet. You should just fire me now.
*Which Number or Response Did You Select?*_____*#2 is the best response*

Statement # Two—I have a couple of people on my staff that just keep me awake at night. They never listen. They just want to do everything their way
*Which Number or Response Did You Select?*_____*#3 is the best response*

Statement # Three— The boss was really in bad mood today. In fact, he/she seems to be in a bad mood almost every day. I hate to be around him/her. I never know if I will get screamed at or patted on the back
*Which Number or Response Did You Select?*_____*#3 is the best response*

Statement # Four—I am getting tired of everyone putting each other down at the meetings. We need to come together as a team. You are pitting us against one another rather than building team play
*Which Number or Response Did You Select?*_____*#4 is the best response*

Statement # Five—Everyone in this organization needs to step up and be more accountable. Senior management doesn't want to hear excuses, they want results
*Which Number or Response Did You Select?*_____*#3 is the best response*

Hopefully, you selected the five best responses. We will discuss the rating scale for *content/message* statements in this section.

If you selected 7 of the 10 best answers, you are responding at a helpful level.

Reviewing the Overall

Helping Communication Response Rating Scale

If a person is going to improve his/her *Helping Communication Skills*, it is important to learn a rating scale that can reveal how you and others are responding to another person. Where a person falls on the rating scale tells you where he/she is functioning when it comes to responding to other people. When developing this **Model**, I decided to go with a rating scale of 1 to 4. I will explain the overall rating system and then discuss how the rating scale relates to the following three areas below.

- Attending (nonverbal) Responses
- Listening/Responding with Respect and Accuracy to a Person's Feelings
- Listening/Responding with Respect and Accuracy to a Person's Message

The *four communication levels* in our rating scale are classified as follows:
A <u>Level One</u> Response is Harmful and Demeaning Communication.

The person responding misses the message completely. He/she takes the speaker away from what he/she is feeling and saying. The person responding:

- makes a person feel like what they are saying and feeling is not important
- completely misses what is being said and takes the conversation in a different direction
- ignores the speaker's feelings and message
- imposes his/her own beliefs and values on the speaker
- dominates the conversation keeping the spotlight on themselves
- changes the accuracy of the speaker's perception of the situation and damages the relationship
- operates as a *magician* (makes problem go away) *swami* (predicts what will happen), *foreman* (work hard and ignore the problem) and *sign painter* (describes the solution or what is wrong so you can move on).

A <u>Level Two</u> Response is Distracting and Ineffective Communication

This response barely touches on the feelings and subject matter of the speaker.

- breaks the speaker's concentration with distracting attending skills
- changes the subject quickly and often
- gives premature or superficial advice before understanding the situation
- responds in a causal or mechanical way-shows a lack of interest
- reflects partial comfort and ignores the feelings of the speaker
- partial response to what the speaker is trying to say
- responds in a questioning way controlling the dialogue (detective)

A <u>Level Three</u> Response is Helpful and Promotes Surface Dialogue

The helper's response focuses on what the speaker is saying and feeling. The person helps another person by:

- being attentive and showing interest in what the speaker has to say
- responding accurately enough to keep speaker's discussion on a surface and interactive level
- responding in a way to keep the speaker on the subject matter
- responding in a way to help the speaker understand his feelings about the situation or issue.
- communicating an acceptance of the speaker's worth
- holding advice and communicating and believing the speaker can solve his/her own problems
- keeping the spotlight on the speaker

A <u>Level Four</u> Response is Helpful and Promotes Deeper Dialogue—Adds Understanding to the Discussion.
The communication enhances a deeper understanding of feelings and subject matter.

The response hits the bull's eye, helping the speaker understand his/her feelings and problem area. The helper:

- reflects a deep interest in the person and what he/she has to say.
- displays good eye contact, facial expressions, posture and proximity
- adds to what the person is saying, increases understanding of feelings, mood and subject matter
- moves from vagueness to clarity
- sharing a relevant experience that increases understanding
- shows complete faith in a person's ability to handle his own situation
- points out discrepancies in the speaker's words and actions
- can talk about what the speaker is feeling in the here and now
- compliments, praises and gives credit to the person
- helps person move to action to achieve plan
- keeps spotlight on person until message is understood at a deeper level
- makes it easier for individuals to solve problems and complete tasks

Sharpening My Attending Skills When Listening to a Person Speak

Your attending skills are the physical expressions, warmth and caring you express when you approach, stand by, sit near and listen to someone speak. Behavior such as eye contact, facial expression, body movement and posture can make one feel important or insignificant. Attending skills reflect the amount of respect one has for another person and can impact that person's self-image. Ineffective attending behavior tends to close off conversation and prohibits relationships from growing. If an individual shares with one person or a group of people, the attending skills reflect the degree of interest shown in what that person is sharing. Effective attending skills reinforce sharing, build relationships and group cohesiveness.

Rating Scale

Levels 3 and 4 Communication Responses

1. <u>Eye contact</u> is directly on speaker all the time
   * Sparkling
   * Wide-eyed
   * Moving with you
   * Alert

2. <u>Facial expression</u> is congruent with the speaker's conversation or feelings
   * Smile when speaker smiles
   * Shows concern when speaker shows concerned
   * Reflects sadness when speaker is sad
   * Laughs when speaker laughs
   * Nods to express agreement
   * Expresses warmth in face

3. <u>Posture and body movement</u> is relaxed and reflects interest
   * Changes position without making a lot of noise
   * Gestures reflect a sign of approval
   * Faces speaker

Levels 2 and 1 Communication Responses

1. <u>Eye contact</u> is on another person or constantly shifting when someone is talking
   * Moving eyes
   * Drooping eyes
   * Closing eyes
   * Looking at watch, floor, etc.

2. <u>Facial expression</u> reflects person is somewhere else or not congruent with the conversation
   * Frowning
   * Shaking head in disagreement
   * Deep thought—mind is somewhere else
   * Head is down as you are texting someone

3. <u>Posture and body movement</u> is distracting and takes spotlight off speaker
   * Slouches
   * Fidgets and squirms
   * Arms closed revealing a lack of interest or judgment
   * Turns away from other person while he/she is speaking
   * Plays with hair, buttons, clothing or other objects
   * Hunches over while sitting
   * Taps foot or thumps fingers

Another area that is important to having good attending skills is being in good physical shape. It takes a lot of energy to be a good listener especially when a session is going for an hour or longer

If your attention begins to lapse after you have been listening to a person talk for a few minutes, you will probably notice some changes in the speaker's behavior. When the speaker suspects that your attention is beginning to drop, he or she is likely to try to recapture your attention, either by talking louder, faster or in a more animated way.

The speaker may also move closer to you or if you are looking in another direction or may move into your field of vision so you will be forced to make eye contact. These are signs that your attending skills are deficient at that time and indicate the speaker is not satisfied with the level of attention that you are giving. The attention we give to individuals impacts attitude, productivity and working relationships.

What are your thoughts on the importance of attending skills?

How have effective attending skills impacted your relationship with others?

There are six tasks that we would like you to master in the attending-skills area.

1. Make appropriate eye contact.

2. Make sure your facial expressions are congruent with the speaker's message.

3. Use appropriate posture to listen and respond.

4. Use body language and gestures that enhance communication.

5. Create space or distance between you and others so it enhances communication.

6. Do not send text messages or talk on your cell phone when someone is speaking to you unless you are gathering information that is relevant to the conversation.

Listening /Responding with Respect and

Accuracy to a Person's Feelings

Why is listening and responding with respect and accuracy to a person's feeling so important in the work place? A Vice President of Human Resources once told me "if people that work here are not thick skinned, they should not work here".

Being able to respond with empathy is a skill that everyone in the organization needs to master. If your position calls for people contact, chances are that every day you will encounter a customer, colleague, direct report or someone who is angry or emotionally upset about something that has happened to them. If you can respond with empathy showing that person you understand his or her feelings, you will diffuse or help the person work through the anger or emotional state and regain their composure. Once this happens, the individual can talk about his or her situation more objectively and make wise decisions.

The fast pace of change is causing more psychological distress with employees. Management needs to know how to respond with empathy to show employees they know how they are feeling. It is also equally important to respond to happy feelings. This will help employees stay in a more productive state of mind.

What are your thoughts on the importance of empathy in the workplace?

How do you feel towards someone who is empathic versus a person who ignores your feelings and uses the big stick to push you? Are all the employees in your organization thick skinned? If you think so, just attack them verbally in a meeting in front of others and see how they react at that moment and afterwards.

We will discuss five exercises to improve your empathy responding skills

- *Exercise # One*—Learn the Two Primary Feeling Categories
- *Exercise # Two*—Learn Six Affect Areas in the Pleasant Category and a Few Feeling Words in Each Area so You Can Describe a Person's Feelings.
- *Exercise #Three*—Identify the Nine Affect Areas in the Unpleasant Category and Learn a Few Feeling Words in Each Area to Describe a Person's Feelings
- *Exercise# Four*-Learn a Phrase that You can Use to Respond with Empathy and Enhance Understanding
- *Exercise# Five*: Learn to Control the Intensity Level of Your Communication

Exercise # One—Learn the <u>Two Primary Feeling Categories</u>

The two primary feeling categories you would place people in would be the **unpleasant state of mind** and **pleasant state of mind**. Many people will fluctuate back and forth in these two states of mind based on what happens to them. However, there are those people who are usually more positive than negative and those more negative than positive. Hopefully, a person doesn't remain in one.

Your job is to help individuals operate in a positive state of mind more than the negative so they can complete work tasks and make logical decisions. People usually don't make good decisions when they are angry or mad. Have you ever made a good decision while mad?

Exercise # Two—Learn the <u>Six Affect Areas</u> in the Pleasant Mind Category and Feeling Words in Each Area You Can Use to Describe a Person's Feelings

We have chosen **six affect areas** that fall in the Pleasant Category. A list of affective adjectives is outlined under these **six affect areas** in *Appendix A* of this manual. This list of adjectives was developed to help you learn words in each **affect area** that can help you describe what a person is feeling when speaking to you. Identify a few words from the **six affect areas** in *Appendix A* that you might use when making an empathic response and write them below.

Pleasant State of Mind—*Six Affect Areas*
<u>Affect Area #1</u>: **Kind**—helpful—loving—friendly—thankful
    Example: Considerate

<u>Affect Area #2</u>: **Curious**—absorbed
    Example: Reflective

<u>Affect Area #3</u>: **Happy**—peaceful
    Example: Calm

<u>Affect Area #4</u>:—**Good-humored**—joking—witty
    Example: Playful

<u>Affect Area #5</u>: **Delighted**—excited
    Example: Giddy

<u>Affect Area #6</u>: **Vigorous**—confident
    Example: strong

Exercise # Three—Learn the <u>Nine Affect Areas</u> in the Unpleasant Category and Feeling Words in Each Area You Can Use to Describe a Person's Feelings

We have chosen **nine affect areas** that fall in the unpleasant state of mind category. A vocabulary list of affective adjectives is outlined under these **nine affect areas** in *Appendix A* of this manual. This list of adjectives was developed to help you learn words that fall in each **affect area** which can help you describe what a person is feeling when speaking to you. Select a few words from the **nine affect areas** in *Appendix A* that you might use to in making an empathic response and write them below.

Unpleasant State of Mind—Nine Affect Areas

<u>Affect Area #1</u>: **Miserable** troubled—hurt—frustrated
  Example: Bothered

<u>Affect Area #2</u>: **Ashamed**—guilty—embarrassed
  Example: Humiliated

<u>Affect Area #3</u>: **Disgusted**—suspicious
  Example: Mistrustful

<u>Affect Area #4</u>: **Weak**—defeated—shy—belittled
  Example: Exhausted

<u>Affect Area #5</u>: **Lonely**—forgotten—left out
  Example: Betrayed

<u>Affect Area #6</u>: **Angry**—hostile—enraged—irritated
  Example: Bitter

<u>Affect Area #7</u>: **Confused**—surprised—astonished
  Example: Dismayed

<u>Affect Area #8</u>: **Sad**—depressed—discouraged
  Example: Dejected

<u>Affect Area #9</u>: **Anxious**—worried
  Example: Tense

Review **Appendix A** and learn feeling words that would fall under each of the **15 affect areas**. Please note that the unpleasant state of mind has more affect areas. Is this because people seem to be in this state of mind more often?

Exercise Four—Learn a Phrase that you can use to respond with empathy and enhance understanding.

Write out the following in regard to the speakers below.

Respond below to this statement "To feel bad, all I have to do is review what has happened in my life. Over the year, I have messed up my marriage with my drinking and now my wife and I are separated".
You feel _____

because _____

Respond below to this statement—"I am depressed. I don't feel like working any more today. I actually work all the time and never take any time off. I deserve a day off once in awhile".
You feel _____

because _____

Respond below to this statement "A lot of times I have been ready to give up—just quit. But if I quit, I might regret it later, maybe even the next day. There are times I can't stand coming here, but there are times I love it. If I only knew how I would like it when training is over
You feel _____

because _____

Respond below to this statement—"I am so excited. We just finished the year and exceeded our profit objectives. I am really hoping for a big bonus and even a good raise in salary".
You feel _____

because _____

Exercise Five: Learn to Control the Intensity Level of Your Communication

When you respond to an individual, you can raise the intensity of your communication by using appropriate adverbs before the adjectives. For example: You can go from saying you feel <u>somewhat angry</u> with your manager to you feel <u>extremely angry </u>with your manager. By choosing the right adverb, you can raise the intensity level of the conversation.

You feel <u>somewhat angry</u> with your manager for embarrassing you.
You feel <u>quite angry</u> with your manager for embarrassing you.
You feel <u>very angry</u> with your manager for embarrassing you.
You feel <u>extremely angry</u> with your manager for embarrassing you.

You feel <u>somewhat sad</u> about Jack getting fired because he didn't deserve it.
You feel <u>quite sad</u> about Jack getting fired because he didn't deserve it.
You feel <u>very sad</u> about Jack getting fired because he didn't deserve it.
You feel <u>extremely sad</u> about Jack getting fired because he didn't deserve it.

You are <u>somewhat excited</u> about you bonus.
You are <u>quite excited</u> about your bonus.
You are <u>very excited </u>about your bonus.
You are <u>extremely excited </u>about your bonus.

Listening /Responding with Respect and

Accuracy to a Person's Message

When listening to a person speak, you will find that a person will focus on about six topics when they are speaking to you. They include:

- Issues, Problems and Challenges Facing Them at Work
- Interpersonal Conflicts and Situations
- Family Issues
- Economic/Financial Issues
- World and Local Events
- Jokes and Stories to Make You Laugh

Your challenge is to sharpen your attending and listening skills so you can respond respectfully and accurately to the message the individual is sending to you. Again, you would use the following scale to rate your responses.

Level One Response—the response takes the person away from his issue /problem or challenge and could change the subject
Level Two Response—Barely touches on what the speaker is saying. The response slightly touches on the message and does not promote discussion of the topic
Level Three Response—Focuses on subject matter and message of speaker at a surface level so the conversation can move forward.
Level Four Response—Focuses on message and adds insight into the message so deeper understanding of the situation or problem occurs.

Tasks that need to be mastered to respond with respect include:
1. Talk adult to adult and not parent to child
2. Be non-judgmental with the individual
3. Use the Task Empowerment Process to help individuals master tasks. The individual then knows you will coaching him/her on certain tasks.
4. Avoid playing the *detective* role of tracking down the facts or grilling an individual. The detective controls the flow of the conversation.
5. Avoid the *magician's* role of making the individual's problem disappear.
6. Avoid the *foreman* role of keeping the person so busy he/she will not be able to think about the problem.
7. Avoid playing the role of the *swami*. The swami knows and predicts what is going to happen.
8. Avoid playing the role of the *drill sergeant*. These people give orders and expect them to be obeyed.

Phrases that can help you clarify a person's message or statement.

Use the phrases below to help you clarify what a person is saying to you.

- You feel.
- From your point of view . . .
- It seems to you . . .
- In your experience . . .
- From where you stand.
- As you see it.
- You think.
- You believe
- What I hear you saying.
- You're (identify the feeling; for example, angry, sad, overjoyed)
- I'm picking up that you
- You mean . . .
- I'm not sure if I'm with you, but
- What I guess I'm hearing is
- Correct me if I'm wrong, but.
- What I'm picking up is
- From where I stand.
- This is what I think I hear you saying . . .
- I somehow sense that maybe you feel . . .
- Is it conceivable that.
- Maybe I'm out to lunch, but.
- Maybe this is a long shot, but.
- I'm not sure if I'm with you, do you mean.
- I'm not certain I understand, you're feeling.
- As I hear it, you . . .
- Let me see if I understand—you.
- I get the impression that . . .

There are three training modules to help you sharpen your attending, listening and responding skills. They include:

Module One—Role-Playing—Triad (three people-one talking, one responding and one rating the person responding)

Module Two: One-on-One Role Playing—Audio/TV

Module Three: Live Group Meeting—Audio/TV

SECTION FOUR

Using the Performance Facilitation and

Helping Communication Model in

One-On-One Sessions/Team Meetings

To Grow Individuals & the Organization

An Outline of Section Four

In section four, we will focus on the following three topics.

- The Importance of One-On-One Meetings

- Using the *Performance Facilitation & Helping Communication Model* in One-On-One Meetings to Help Individuals Understand Themselves, The Challenges They Face and Develop and Execute Plans that Will Meet Their Future Challenges

- Using the *Performance Facilitation & Helping Communication Model to* Build Team Cohesiveness and Team Play to Meet Plan-Close the Gap

The Importance of Sharing and Having One-On-One Meetings

I have conducted over 2,500 One-On-One sessions with executives, managers, supervisors and non-exempts since 1982. When I asked these individuals, "What was the number one factor that impacted your performance at work?" Their answer always centered on the working relationship and communication they had with their manager or boss. The majority said they had two One-On-One meetings a year. One was at the beginning of the year and the other was at the end of the year.

Through further discussion, I identified the following reasons for the lack of continuous One-On-One meetings:
- My company emphasized a planning meeting at the first of the year and a performance review at the end of the year.
- Managers do not like giving performance reviews.
- Performance reviews are confrontational and tear down working relationships.
- One-On-One meetings are time consuming so why not have group sessions instead or e-mail each other?
- One-On-One meetings demand too much preparation and can be an aggravation when you are busy.
- Unit leaders are not adequately trained to conduct One-On-One sessions.
- People are paid to make decisions and do their job; they should not depend on their unit leader to tell them what to do.
- One-On-One meetings are always perceived to be performance reviews and not developmental sessions.

Some of the conflicts that managers and direct reports encountered when working with each other One-On-One included:
- Control issues
- Lack of trust
- Personality differences
- Understanding each other's needs and wants
- Understanding expectations from each other
- Understanding the capabilities to do specific tasks and projects
- Understanding who is accountable for what
- Taking the time to build a working relationship
- Behaving as performance inhibitors rather than performance facilitators
- Disrespectful behavior
- Being defensive, afraid to discuss issues and admit making mistakes
- Lacking the ability to respond with empathy
- Poor communication

Many CEOs seem convinced that their communication carries the biggest weight in the organization when it comes to impacting employees. A study of 164 CEOs in Fortune 500 companies by A. Forster Higgins & Company revealed that 95% of them believe their communication affects employee satisfaction and 75% felt their communication influenced employee job performance. The study reported that there was no evidence that communication from CEOs in large companies significantly affects employee behavior. A high-level leader can make a positive impression by being visible and walking around the company, but this behavior does not make as much of an impact on each employee as a CEO might think. In most companies, it is too difficult for top leaders to know every employee well, so they need to rely on an effective management team to do the communicating.

There is a wealth of supporting evidence to show that increasing the position power of managers and frontline supervisors influences employees more and builds organization cohesiveness. In the book *Communicating Change*, T.J. and Sandra Larkin[4] revealed several research studies showing the importance of empowering managers and supervisors to manage the talent in the organization.

A study by Karlene Roberts[5] and Charles O'Reilly revealed that when an employee perceives that their manager or supervisor has more power in the organization, it increases:
- Trust in the supervisor and manager
- Desire for communication with the supervisor and manager
- Belief in the accuracy of information delivered by the supervisor and manager.

Paul Nystrom[6], a researcher studying commitment within organizations, discovered that the quality of the relationship with one's boss is three times more powerful in predicting commitment to the organization.

Studies by Brad Whitworth[7] of Hewlett-Packard indicated that when managers communicate effectively, employees are more satisfied with all aspects of their work life. A positive communicative relationship with the supervisor generates higher opinions of:

• Corporate image and policy	• Overall management	• Training
• Working conditions	• Operating efficiency	• Pay and benefits

The more I listened and researched the topic of One-On One sessions, the more I discovered that many managers do not have a *leadership development and performance management system* they can use to transform their direct reports into leaders in their fields and the unit/organization into the best in it's functional area or industry. Many unit leaders shoot from the hip and put off *One-On-One* sessions. Can you imagine a football or basketball coach not preparing his players to play against the competition? A coach (team unit leader) must create an offensive and defensive system that turns his players into All Americans and provides the unit/organization the opportunity to become a championship team.

I have developed a leadership development and performance management development system that team unit leaders can use to transform direct reports into leaders in their fields and the unit into a championship organization. The system is called *The Triangle Team Leadership Model: Becoming the Best in Our Field*. I have developed three work books and several assessment surveys to help team unit leaders execute the *Model*. They are:
- *Becoming the Best in Our Field: The Team Unit Leader's Plan*
- *Becoming the Best in Our Field: The Unit and Team Members; Plans*
- *Sharpening My One-On-One Performance Facilitation & Helping Communication Skills*

The assessments include:
- The Leadership & Management Analysis Survey (six assessments)
- The Helping Assessment Survey
- The Performance Facilitation Assessment Survey
- The Route 66 Job Satisfaction Survey
- The Career Management Competency Survey (100 items)
- The Self Actualization Needs Survey

One-On-One sessions with direct reports are key to solidifying the vision, mission and objectives of both the company and team unit. Team unit leaders can't manage groups of people but can only manage individuals One-On-One. Team unit leaders should aim at working with and through their direct reports to transform them into leaders in their field and the unit and organization into the best in it's industry. One-On One sessions can also build team cohesiveness and team play by solving interpersonal issues in a private setting.

You can go to www.mulliganassoc.com to learn more about the system and how Mulligan & Associates can help team unit leaders execute it with direct reports.

Notes

Using the *Performance Facilitation & Helping Communication Model* in One-On-One Sessions to Help Individuals Understand Themselves, Their Challenges and Develop & Execute Plans that will Meet the Challenges

(Helping Customers and Fellow Employees Succeed)

The Three Stages of the Performance Facilitation Process		
Stage One **Slow Pace**	*Stage Two* **Moderate Pace**	*Stage Three* **Very Fast Pace**
Building A Working and Sharing Relationship	Dialogue, Understanding and Establishing a Plan	Executing the Plan and Achieving Results
• A Common Ground	• *Δ Team Leadership Model*–Challenges	• Gap Closure System—The 4 M's
• Trust	• *Gap Closure System*–Objectives	• One-on-One Meetings
• Empathy	• *Gap Closure System*—Tasks	• Positive Reinforcement
• Respect	• *Task Empowerment Process*-Prepare	• Constructive Confrontation

Listening

Attending   Responding

The Three Helping Communication Skills

We will discuss the three stages of the *Performance Facilitation Process* and the importance of mastering the *three helping communication skills*.

In order to help someone discuss and understand an issue or problem and develop and execute a solution, you need to be functioning at a competent level when executing the *Performance Facilitation Process* and the *three helping communication skills* (attending, listening and responding). If every unit leader/employee in an organization can master these two parts of the *Performance Facilitation & Helping Communication Model*, they will help build All American employees and many Championship teams.

The Performance Facilitation Process & Helping Communication Skills

We will discuss each of the three stages of the *Performance Facilitation Process* and then review the *three helping communication skills*.

Stage One of the Process-(Slow Pace)
One-on-One Meetings
Building A Working and Sharing Relationship
A common ground Trust Empathy Respect

If you want to build a *working and sharing relationship* with individuals or direct reports, there are at least four steps you need to take.

The <u>first step</u> would be to develop a *common bond* or some kind of *common ground* with the individual. You should start out by discussing non threatening topics. Later, you can move to more personal topics when people trust and feel they have a relationship with you. On pages 75 to 79, there are some informational surveys that team unit leaders can use at some point to learn more about their direct reports. On page 80, we have developed a 25 Issue Survey that a team unit leader can use to discover what issues are most important to direct reports. Then the unit leader can start out discussing the issues most important to each direct report.

The <u>second step</u> is to build *trust* between one another. No one wants to discuss personal issues or express how they feel about someone or the organization if they feel it will be held against them. In many organizations today, there are many people who are operating in an unpleasant state of mind because someone put them there and they allowed that person to put them there. The question is who in the organization can they *trust* to discuss their hurt. How many organizations are operating at half speed today because their employees are upset and not focused?

The <u>third step</u> is to sharpen your *attending and listening skills* so you can *respond* with *empathy*. You will find that the more you can respond with empathy and identify what a person is feeling, the sooner your working and sharing relationship with someone will take off.

The <u>fourth step</u> is to treat direct reports and other employees with *respect.* You have to believe people can operate as a self manager and solve their own problems. You don't want to act as a detective, magician, swami, foreman and sign painter.

Many team unit leaders want to start and stay in the Third Stage of this Process.

What many team unit leaders don't understand is that if you don't build a strong working relationship in the beginning with individuals, it will be more difficult to push and confront them when the going gets tough. You want to tell them when the tough times come, the tough get going. The dedication to the cause and each other will help team units and organizations succeed.

Gathering Information about Direct Reports

Name of Direct Report

Nickname:

Birth Place and Date:

Their Family.

Spouse—Name and Occupation:

Children—Name(s), Age(s) and Information

About The Individual

Where were you born?

Where did you grow up?

What do you like to do when you are not working?:

What is your career aspiration?

How has the company helped you grow? In which areas can the company help you now?

What would you do to make our organization better? Our division? Our dept?
See survey on pages 76 to 78

What does our culture look like to you today? See survey on page 79

What are the discussion topics on page 80 most important to you?

High School and College information about Direct Reports

Indicate highest degree completed

High School:	FR	SOPH	JR	SR
College:	FR	SOPH	JR	SR

Vocational School: Certification: _____

Graduate School: Degree Received: _____

	High School	College	College	College
Name of School and Location:				
Dates of Attendance:				
Type of student				
College Major/ Minor Studies				
Favorite Subject(s):				
Offices Held, Extra activities				
Honors and awards				

Professional Certifications:

_____

Future Targeted Degree and Training:

_____

_____

Listed below is a survey direct reports can fill out. You and your direct reports can discuss their evaluation. You can learn how they view the organization.

40 Major Challenges Facing Our Organization	Please rate the following challenges in terms of how effective our organization is managing them. Scale 0-10 0—not effective 10—extremely effective
1. Creating change agendas that are needed, communicating the agendas and gaining commitment to implement them.	
2. Developing a Leadership Empowerment and Expert Program to determine when to empower employees.	
3. Attracting, selecting and retaining employees who will help us become number one.	
4. Establishing a pay for performance incentive plan.	
5. Increasing profit and shareholder value.	
6. Developing a company vision, mission, objectives and a plan and executing the plan so we are successful.	
7. Maintaining excellent relations with present customers while increasing our customer base.	
8. Determining what businesses we want to be in.	
9. Identifying our market niche and increasing share.	
10. Developing a One-On-One management program to increase individual productivity, performance and leadership so employees and the company become the best in their fields.	
11. Pursuing a cause or purpose that will unify, excite and reward everyone in the organization.	
12. Increasing quality of products/service while managing costs.	
13. Training employees how to function as skilled performance facilitators to bring out the best in themselves and others.	
14. Keeping up with the latest technology to remain competitive.	
15 Satisfying and meeting the needs of the workforce so they can better focus on achieving tasks and objectives.	
16. Building a unified workforce	
17. Containing health care costs and decreasing absenteeism at work.	
18. Building a "Competitive Intelligence and Learning Center" to grow individuals and beat the competition.	
19. Deciding whether to manufacture or outsource products.	
20. Establishing a participation management style to include all employees in the business planning process.	
21. Constantly striving to beat local and global competition to be number one in the marketplace.	
22. Defining and living company values.	

23. Using the expertise of retired employees.	
24. Evaluating how we communicate to each other in the organization and developing a plan to improve our helping communication skills	
25. Reducing costs by hiring a combination of full time, part time and temporary employees.	
26. Establishing a career development program for all employees.	
27. Identifying performance facilitating behaviors and working with employees to turn them into everyday habits.	
28. Developing a merger and acquisition strategy to grow.	
29. Managing occupational safety and health.	
30. Establishing a program that reduces anger and lawsuits in the workplace.	
31. Developing a competency base program and creating a talent pool to be used through the organization.	
32. Managing downsizing and restructuring without reducing the enthusiasm and commitment of the workforce.	
33. Supplying the resources needed to compete and grow the company while maintaining a meaningful work environment.	
34. Developing a team leadership model so all employees know when and how to step up as leaders.	
35. Defining what is politically and ethically correct in the organization.	
36 The Board of Directors and senior management team working together to lead the company	
37. Establishing a win-win situation between the union and management.	
38. Identifying future team unit leaders and building a leadership farm system to train them	
39. Helping employees balance work and personal life.	
40. Marketing and selling our company to the stock analysts or public.	
TOTAL POINTS	=
AVERAGE SCORE (DIVIDE BY 40 TO OBTAIN SCORE)	=

How employees perceive the company culture—A culture is defined as a group of people who agree on goals and objectives, and establish customs, beliefs, traditions and norms of behavior which everyone follows. Employees imitate senior management, so it is important that the guidelines established in the company are clearly stated, modeled and reinforced. The question every company needs to ask itself is "Will our present culture promote team cohesiveness and motivate everyone to achieve objectives that will make us champions in our field?"

Ask your direct reports to circle the six words that describe your company culture.
- Adhocracy (management by committee)
- Authoritarian (paternalistic)
- Always Putting Out Fires
- Political
- Caring
- Hire and Fire
- Fat Cats
- Bureaucratic
- Friendly/stakeholder oriented
- Production oriented
- Punitive/demeaning
- Conformists
- Hierarchical
- Quality conscious
- Competitive
- Innovative/creative/forward looking
- Risk-Avoidance
- Customer focused
- Work hard—Play hard
- Elitist
- Status conscious
- Divided
- Diversity oriented
- Technocratic
- Egalitarian (cooperative)
- Open minded/make changes when necessary
- Traditional
- Profit focused
- Employee focused

Rating the Issues to be Discussed in a One-On-One Meeting

Listed below are twenty-five issues that a team unit leader and his or her direct report could discuss with each other. The team unit leader can ask each direct report to rate the 25 items below in regard to the importance it has to them. Then the team unit leader can rate the 25 items in regard to the importance it has to him/her. Discuss the ratings to see if you both can come to an agreement on what is most important to both of you and then discuss them.

Your Perception of the most important issues to discuss with your manager is crucial. Please rate below, 1 to 25, 1 being high and 25 being low, the issues that you think are the most important items to discuss with your manager:

____ How profitability helps everyone in the organization
____ Being customer focused
____ My career and personal background
____ Balance of work and my personal life
____ How I can increase my value to the department and the organization
____ My knowledge skills, talent and experience and how I can use them to grow on the job
____ Areas where I need personal and professional growth
____ A plan to grow personally and professionally
____ What we can expect from each other
____ The vision, mission and performance objectives of the organization, department and division
____ My performance objectives and plans—striving to be a performance leader
____ Projects and tasks for which I am responsible and accountable
____ What I am empowered to do
____ How I can help others in the organization
____ My career development and advancement
____ How I can be a team leader, follower, and builder
____ How to enjoy and make work meaningful
____ My emotional well being and how I handle stress
____ My health and fitness goals, e.g., to exercise, lose weight, stop smoking
____ My overall health and energy level
____ How I can increase my expert, personal and position power
____ Having a winning and positive attitude
____ My Championship objectives, plan and progress being made
____ How the department and I can become the best in the field
____ Performance incentives (pay, vacation, bonuses, promotion, etc.)

Stage Two of the Process-Moderate Pace

One-on-One Meetings

Dialogue, Understanding and Establishing a Plan

—Δ Team Leadership Model-The Challenges
—Gap Closure System-Objectives
—Gap Closure System-Tasks
—Task Empowerment Process

If you want to help customers, direct reports or fellow employees *discuss and understand challenge(s)* and assist them in *developing and executing the appropriate plan* (achieving objectives) to meet the challenge(s), there are three steps you should take.

The <u>first step</u> would be to sit down One-On-One with your customer, direct reports, colleague and boss and discuss the Δ Team Leadership Model: Meeting Challenges and Becoming the Best. You want to display excellent *attending skills* so the person knows you are interested in what he/she has to say. You should *listen* to the person when he/she discusses his/her challenges. Your accurate responses to the person's feelings and message will help identify the key challenge(s) the individual faces. With more accurate responding, the individual will eventually have an *in-depth understanding* of the challenge(s) he/she faces at this time.

To help someone understand their challenge or situation, you can *self disclose* a similar experience that you had in your life that will shed more light and insight to their situation. It is through this *in-depth understanding* that the person you are helping can develop wise and appropriate plans (setting objectives) to solve their situation, problem or challenge.

The <u>second step</u> would be to execute the *Gap Closure System.* A person needs to understand what his/her challenge is today and what it will take to meet the challenge. You need to help the individual set an objective, that if met, would help them meet their challenge and Close the Gap-solve the problem.

The <u>third step</u> would be to identify the tasks that must be achieved to meet the objective (s). (Close the Gap between where you are and where you need to be-to meet the challenge). The *Task Empowerment Process* can be used to prepare a person to execute all the tasks. The Challenge Solving Model can be used in Stage Two of the Process.

The Challenge Solving Model

The *Challenge Solving Model* is outlined below and used in **Stage Two** of the *Performance Facilitation Process*

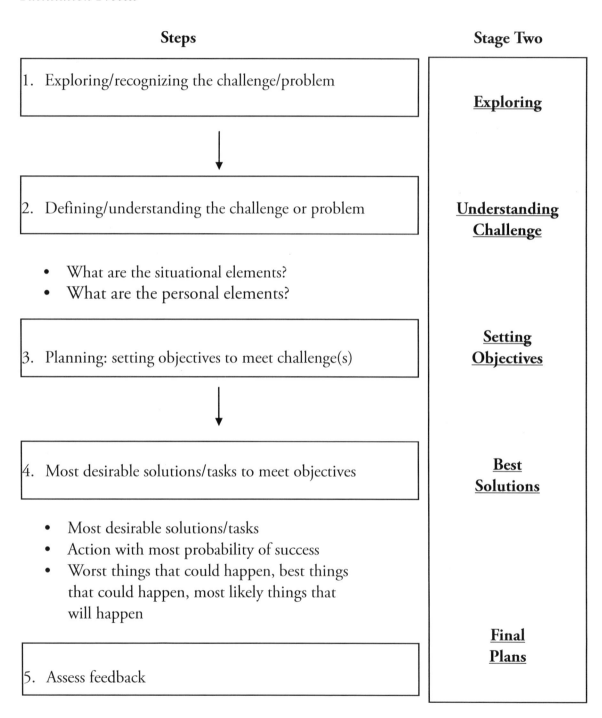

Steps

1. Exploring/recognizing the challenge/problem	

Stage Two

Exploring

2. Defining/understanding the challenge or problem

Understanding Challenge

- What are the situational elements?
- What are the personal elements?

3. Planning: setting objectives to meet challenge(s)

Setting Objectives

4. Most desirable solutions/tasks to meet objectives

Best Solutions

- Most desirable solutions/tasks
- Action with most probability of success
- Worst things that could happen, best things that could happen, most likely things that will happen

Final Plans

5. Assess feedback

Stage Three of the Process

Stage Three
One-on-One Meetings
Executing the Plan and Achieving Results
Gap Closure System—The 4 M's Motivational One-On-One Meetings Positive Reinforcement Constructive Confrontation

If you want to help an individual *execute his/her plan and achieve the results* they want, there are four steps you need to take.

In <u>Step One</u>, you and your direct reports should meet One-On-One each month and execute the *Gap Closure System* focusing on the 4 M's.
    — *Monitor* your plan
    — *Measure* your task efforts and action solutions
    — *Modify* your plans based on new information
    — *Meet* the objectives in your plan and *Close the Gap.*

In <u>Step Two</u>, team unit leaders should do things in One-On-One meetings to motivate their direct reports to use 100% of their potential. Listed below is a list of motivators that Frederick Hertzberg identified when doing his research.

What Satisfies Employees	**What Motivates Employees**
Fair company policies and procedures	Challenge
Effective supervision	Achievement
Positive relationships with supervisors	Recognition
Excellent working conditions	Responsibility
Competitive salaries	Advancement
Productive relationships with peers	Growth
Balance between personal life and work	AdditionalCompensation
Excellent relationships with direct reports	
Status	
Security	

The Society of Human Resource Members (SHRM) released a study in the Sunday November 6th, 2011 *Chicago Tribune* showing that job security, communication and engagement with management and using their talent were the top satisfiers.

In the *Triangle Team Leadership Model: Becoming the Best in Our Field.* we use challenge (a cause) as the motivator to unite, excite and grow employees.

<u>In Step Three,</u> team unit leaders should use *positive reinforcement* communication with their direct reports in their One-On-One and team meetings. Just as it is important to point out discrepancies in performance, it is important to recognize excellent work and provide positive feedback on a timely basis. When an individual completes a task or project, meets predetermined objectives or behaves in a certain way to facilitate performance in others, the person should be complimented or recognized for their behavior or performance.

Positive reinforcement should be done on an intermittent basis. This means people should be rewarded or praised at different times without always expecting it. If we reward or praise someone every day, the person becomes satiated. In other words, compliments will not mean as much. The problem we have in the work place today is that people aren't praised or recognized enough.

In <u>Step four,</u> we advocate team unit leaders using constructive confrontation that is not punitive and cruel. Constructive confrontation helps individuals examine the inconsistencies in what they say they are going to do and what they actually do. The focus is on getting people to do what they say they will do.

The model emphasizes that you should earn the right to confront and this is done by building a strong relationship early. This is why we say team unit leaders need to start in *Stage One* of the *Performance Facilitation Process* and move to *Stage Three (the action zone)* after a working relationship has been formed.

However, there is a time when team unit leaders should start in *Stage Three* rather than *Stage One*. If you inherit your staff and find several are disrespectful to you, it would be smart to meet with each direct report right away in One-On One sessions and confront those that are disrespectful. Some times you have to be direct with people or confront them to get their attention. A team member's role is to help the unit leader be successful and vice versa.

In conclusion, confrontation can be damaging to working relations if it isn't handled at the right time and in a professionally manner. Team unit leaders or helpers need to be sensitive to how they confront. Again you want to communicate the message to a person that you are not upset with them personally but you are disappointed in the fact that they are not doing what they said they would do.

You need to continue functioning at a 3 level or higher on all three communication skills (attending, listening and responding) when putting individuals through the *Three Stages* of the *Performance Facilitation Process.*

Using the *Performance Facilitation & Helping Communication Model to* Build Team Cohesiveness and Team Play to Meet Plan or Close the Gap

The Three Stages of the Performance Facilitation Process		
Stage One **Slow Pace**	*Stage Two* **Moderate Pace**	*Stage Three* **Very Fast Pace**
Building A Working and Sharing Relationship	Dialogue, Understanding and Establishing a Plan	Executing the Plan and Achieving Results
• A Common Ground • Trust • Empathy • Respect	• *Δ Team Leadership Model*-Challenges • *Gap Closure System*-Objectives • *Gap Closure System*—Tasks • *Task Empowerment Process-Prepare*	• Gap Closure System—The 4 M's • One-on-One Meetings • Positive Reinforcement • Constructive Confrontation

Listening

Attending   Responding

The Three Helping Communication Skills

If team unit members want to build team cohesiveness, identify the challenges his/her unit faces and develop and achieve "best in the field" objectives with their direct reports to meet challenges, there are seven steps a unit leader should take.

In Step One, unit leaders should learn about the *Achievement Motivation Program* and use it to facilitate sharing and build team cohesiveness and a championship team. An outline of the *Achievement Motivation Program* is discussed on the next page.

In Step Two, unit leaders should teach or have someone teach the *Performance Facilitation & Helping Communication Model* to their direct reports. It's important that all employees understand how to use the *Performance Facilitation Process* and know how to attend, listen and respond to customers and fellow workers. If employees are functioning below a 3 on the performance facilitation and helping communication rating scale, the unit leader will discover that customers will not be treated as well and there will be more rudeness and incivility in the work place.

Executing the Team Achievement Motivation Program

A team unit leader can use the *Team Achievement Motivation Model* to build team unity, and motivate direct reports to establish and meet "best in our field" objectives for themselves and the unit. The *seven activities* in the *Model* include:

Activity One—The key to building working relationships is *learning to share.*

We will discuss the importance of sharing and why individuals don't share. We will ask each member to share what they liked to be called and something about themselves that is not threatening.

Activity Two—Members will *share some of their successes* and *meaningful experiences* in life and at work. We will ask each team member to share some of their successes as well as some of their meaningful experiences in their life.

Activity Three—After team members discuss some of their successes and experiences, we will ask team mates to *identify* each person's *strengths* as they know them at this time. Each team member will be put under the spot light and the other team members will tell that person what they see as their strengths.

Activity Four—Team members should develop *"best in the field"* objectives for the unit and themselves. If these objectives are met, it will transform each team member into a leader in their field and the unit into the best in it's industry.

Activity Five—Team members should share how they plan to *use their talent* to help the unit be successful. We will track the team's success on a monthly basis and develop a team resume so members can see the results of their effort.

Activity Six—Each team member should meet One-On-One with their unit leader and execute The *Task Empowerment Process* which helps each member become an expert in completing the tasks necessary to meet the "best in our field" objectives.

Activity Seven—Members can *build up each others confidence base* by asking each person at the team meetings to discuss how they contributed to the team's success this month. Then members can say something positive about the person when he/she quits talking. The team unit should meet twice a month to discuss how the team as a whole is meeting it's "best in the field" objectives.

In <u>Step Three,</u> each team unit leader should take the *Mulligan Leadership Analysis Survey* (six assessment surveys) to learn where he/she might need to grow to be a more effective team unit leader and One-On-One manager. He/she then can ask direct reports to take it and then go over their results. This gives the unit leader a chance to place direct reports in two leadership pipelines—the management development pipeline and the expert non-management pipeline.

In <u>Step Four,</u> unit leaders should teach direct reports the three stages of the *Performance Facilitation Process.* It is important to discuss the importance of moving from Stage One to Stage Two to Stage Three. The unit leader can discuss the dimensions in each *Stage.* This *Process* gives unit leaders and employees a three stage system they can use to help fellow employees.

In <u>Step Five,</u> unit leaders should teach or have someone teach direct reports how to function at a 3 or higher on their attending and responding skills. If a person doing the teaching is not functioning at a 3, then it would be difficult for that person to help others operate at a 3 level.

In <u>Step Six,</u> unit leaders should continue to meet One-On-One with each direct report every month to execute the 4 M's, provide positive reinforcement and constructive confrontation. It is the combination of face to face One-On-One and team meetings that will energize and keep everyone on track to meet the :best in our field" objectives and future challenges as a unit.

In <u>Step Seven,</u> unit leaders should execute some of the ideas of Lloyd McGinnis on bringing out the best in people on the next page.

McGinnis' 12 Rules for Bringing out the Best in People

Lloyd McGinnis[8] wrote *How to Bring out the Best in People*. He developed 12 rules a unit leader should follow. They are:

- Expect the best from people you lead.
  Believe that people can become and be the best in their field

- Make a thorough study of the other person's needs
  Execute Maslow's Hierarchy of Needs Theory-must meet one's survival security and belonging needs before he/she can become and be

- Establish high standards for excellence.
  Setting growth benchmarks and adhering to them.

- Create an environment where failure is not fatal.
  Allowing "mulligans"—learning from our mistakes.

- If you are going anywhere near where you want to go, climb on other people's bandwagons.
  Establishing a common direction.

- Employ models to encourage success.
  Provide individual examples, stories, or experience.

- Recognize and applaud achievement.
  Take the time to put the spotlight on others.

- Employ a mixture of positive and negative reinforcement.
  Teach people to avoid certain behaviors, not to avoid you.

- Appeal to the competitive urge.
  Competition can excite and bring people together

- Place a premium on collaboration.
  Build an allegiance to each other.

- Build into the group an allowance for storms.
  Let people ventilate in the one-on-one sessions.

- Take steps to keep your own motivation high.
  You should strive to be a leader in your field and help others meet that objective.

Appendix A-Broadening My Vocabulary

Most people have a very limited vocabulary when it come to responding to others. Review this list and pick out five or six words in each category that you might want to use when responding to others about their feelings and message. You can practice these words until they become a natural part of your vocabulary. Copyright © 2012 Michael V. Mulligan

Person in a Pleasant Affective State

Kind-Helpful-Loving-Friendly-Thankful

admired	adored	affectionate	agreeable
altruistic	amiable	amorous	appreciative
aroused	benevolent	big-hearted	brotherly
caring	charitable	cherished	comforting
compassionate	compatible	congenial	conscientious
considerate	cooperative	cordial	dedicated
dependable	devoted	diligent	empathic
fair	faithful	fatherly	fond
forgiving	friendly	generous	genuine
gentle	gallant	giving	good
gracious	grateful	helpful	honest
honorable	humane	idolizing	indebted to
involved	just	kind	longing for
long-suffering	loving	mellow	merciful
mindful	nice	obliging	open
optimistic	passionate	patient	neighborly
respectful	rewarded	sensitive	sharing
sincere	sociable	soft-hearted	straightforward
sympathetic	tender	thoughtful	tolerant
treasured	trustful	unassuming	understanding
unselfish	warm-hearted		

Curious-Absorbed

analyzing	attentive	concentrating	considering
contemplating	curious	diligent	engrossed
imaginative	inquiring	inquisitive	investigating
occupied	pondering	puzzled	questioning
reasoning	reflecting	searching	thoughtful
weighing	wrapped up		

Happy-Peaceful

accepted	amused	at ease	blissful
brilliant	calm	carefree	charmed
cheerful	clear	comfortable	complete
contented	delighted	ecstatic	elated
enjoying	excellent	fantastic	fine
fit	full	giddy	glad
glorious	good	gratified	great
happy	in high spirits	inspired	joyous
jubilant	laughing	lighthearted	magnificent
marvelous	optimistic	overjoyed	peaceful
pleasant	pleased	poised	proud
refreshed	rejoicing	relaxed	relieved
renewed	revived	safe	satiated
satisfied	serene	settled	smiling
soothed	splendid	sunny	superb
sweet	terrific	thrilled	tickled
tremendous	wholesome	wonderful	

Playful-Joking-Witty

agreeable	amusing	breezy	clever
easygoing	free and easy	frisky	fun-loving
funny	genial	good-humored	happy-go-lucky
hearty	hospitable	humorous	joking
jovial	jolly	lighthearted	mischievous
original	lively	quick-witted	smart
sociable	sparkling	spontaneous	sportive
sprightly	spry	turned on	uninhibited
vivacious			

Interested-Excited

active	alert	aroused	attracted to
bubbly	bustling	busy	challenged
delighted	eager	enthusiastic	excited
exuberant	fascinated	flustered	impatient
impressed with	inspired	involved	keyed up
quickened	resourceful	responsive	spurred on
stimulated	Tantalized	thrilled	

Vigorous-Strong-Confident

able-bodied	accomplished	adaptable	adequate
adventurous	alive	ambitious	assertive
assured	blessed	boastful	bold
brave	capable	certain	clever
cocky	competent	competitive	confident
courageous	daring	determined	dignified
dynamic	effective	efficient	encouraged
energetic	equal to the task	favored	fearless
firm	fit	forceful	fortunate
gifted	Hardy	healthy	in control
important	independent	intelligent	keen
lion-hearted	Lucky	macho	mighty
peppy	potent	pumped	prosperous
qualified	powerful	reliable	responsible
secure	self-confident	self-controlled	self-reliant
sharp	shrewd	skillful	smart
solid	spirited	stable	strong
sturdy	suited	sure	successful
together	tough	triumphant	victorious
vigorous	well off	swell suited	wired
wise			

Unpleasant Affective States

Miserable-Troubled-Hurt-Frustrated

abused	aching	afflicted	awful
battered	bothered	bruised	burdened
clumsy	crabby	cramped	cut to the heart
deprived	desolate	desperate	despairing
destitute	dismal	displeased	dissatisfied
distressed	disturbed	divided	dreadful
futile	harassed	hassled	hemmed in
hindered	horrible	imprisoned	jammed up
loaded down	lost	lousy	mistreated
oppressed	pathetic	peeved	perturbed
pitiful	poor	pressured	pulled apart
restless	ridiculous	rotten	ruined
sore	stabbed	strained	strangled
suffering	swamped	temperamental	terrible
threatened	thwarted	tormented	trapped
tortured	uneasy	unfortunate	unhappy
unlucky	unsatisfied	unsure	upset
wiped out	wounded	wretched	

Ashamed-Guilty-Embarrassed

apologetic	awkward	blamed	branded
chagrined	cheapened	condemned	conscience-stricken
contrite	degraded	denounced	disapproved of
disgraced	dishonored	disreputable	doomed
embarrassed	evasive	exposed	foolish
humbled	humiliated	in a bind	in trouble
judged	punished	put down	rebuked
red-faced	regretful	remorseful	ridiculous
roasted	shamed	sheepish	silly
slammed	sorry	wicked	wrong

Disgusted-Suspicious

Arrogant
callous
cynical
derisive
despising
detesting
disgusted
displeased
distrustful
dogmatic
doubting
envious
grudging
hesitant
jealous
loathing
mistrustful
nauseated
nonchalant
offended
pompous
queasy
repulsed
revolted
sickened
skeptical
sneering
wary

Weak-Defeated-Shy-Belittled

all in
at the mercy of
bashful
bent
broken-down
chicken-hearted
cowardly
crippled
crushed
deflated
demeaned
dependent
dominated
done-for
drained
drowsy
exhausted
failing
fatigued
feeble
fragile
frail
hungry
helpless
imperfect
impotent
inadequate
incapable
incompetent
ineffective
inefficient
inept
inferior
insecure
insulted
intimidated
laughed at
needy
neglected
no good
paralyzed
Powerless
puny
put down
run down
scoffed at
self-conscious
shattered
small
smothered
spineless
squelched
stifled
strained
tearful
timid
tired
troubled
unable
not ambitious
unfit
unsure of self
unqualified
unstable
unworthy
useless
vulnerable
walked on
washed up
weak
whipped
wimpy
worthless
yellow

Lonely-Forgotten-Left Out

abandoned	alienated	alone	betrayed
bored	cast aside	cheated	deserted
discarded	disliked	disowned	empty
excluded	forsaken	friendless	hated
hollow	homeless	homesick	ignored
isolated	jilted	left out	lonely
lonesome	lost	neglected	ostracized
outcast	overlooked	rebuffed	rejected
scorned	secluded	shunned	slighted
snubbed	stranded	taken lightly	ugly
uninvited	unimportant	unwanted	unwelcome

Angry-Hostile-Enraged-Irritated

aggravated	aggressive	agitated	angry
annoyed	aroused	belligerent	bitter
boiling	bristling	brutal	bullying
burned	contrary	cool	cranky
critical	cross	cruel	disagreeable
displeased	enraged	ferocious	fierce
fighting	fired up	frenzied	exasperated
fuming	furious	harsh	hateful
heartless	hostile	incensed	indignant
inflamed	infuriated	irked	irritated
mad	mean	out of sorts	outraged
perturbed	provoked	pushy	quarrelsome
raving	ready to explode	rebellious	resentful
revengeful	ruffled	sarcastic	spiteful
steamed	stern	strung out	stormy
unkind	Vindictive	violent	vicious

Confused-Surprised-Astonished

aghast	air-headed	amazed	appalled
astonished	astounded	awed	awestruck
baffled	bewildered	bowled over	breathless
changeable	dazed	dismayed	disorganized
distracted	doubtful	dumfounded	emotional
forgetful	gripped	horrified	in doubt
jarred	jolted	mixed up	muddled
mystified	overpowered	overwhelmed	perplexed
puzzled	rattled	ruffled	shocked
speechless	staggered	startled	stunned
swamped	taken aback	torn	trapped
tricked	uncertain		

Sad-Depressed-Discouraged

below par	bereaved	blue	brooding
broken-hearted	burned out	bummed out	dejected
demolished	depressed	despondent	destroyed
disappointed	discouraged	down-and-out	downhearted
dreary	drooping	dull	falling apart
forlorn	gloomy	glum	grief-stricken
grieved	heavy-hearted	hopeless	in the dumps
let down	lifeless	low	melancholy
moody	moping	mournful	oppressed
pained	pessimistic	sad	serious
shredded	solemn	sorrowful	tearful
troubled	unhappy	weary	woeful

Afraid-Tense-Worried

agonizing	alarmed	anxious	apprehensive
boxed in	cautious	concerned	cornered
disturbed	dreading	edgy	fearful
frantic	frightened	hesitant	horrified
in a cold sweat	jittery	jumpy	on edge
panicky	petrified	nervous	numb
quaking	quivering	restless	scared
shaken	suffocated	terrified	trembling
troubled	up tight	uncomfortable	uneasy

Appendix B—Bibliography

1. Alan Loy McGinnis. *Bringing Out the Best in People. Augsburg Press. Choice Books 2006.*

2. Carkhuff, R.R. *Helping and Human Relations. A Primer for Lay and Professional Helpers. Vol. 2. Practice and Research. New York Rinehart and Winston, 1969.*

3. Gazda, Asbury, Balzer, Childers and Walters. *Human Relations Development: A Manual for Educators.* Fourth Edition. Allyn and Bacon, 1990.

4. T.J. Larkin and Sandra Larkin. *Communicating Change.* McGraw Hill, 1994.

5. Karlene Roberts and Charles O'Reilley. *"Working for a Powerful Supervisor" Communicating Change.* McGraw Hill, 1994.

6. Paul Nystrom. "Organization Commitment" *Communicating Change.* McGraw Hill, 1994.

7. Brad Whitworth. "Poor Communication with a Supervisor Means Lower Job Satisfaction". *Communicating Change.* McGraw Hill, 1994.

8. Alan Loy McGinnis. *Bringing Out the Best in People. Augsburg Press. Choice Books 2006.*